Ghosts Of Buffalo

Ghosts Of Buffalo

Hauntings, Mysteries, And Witchcraft In The Nickel City

Tim Shaw

Schiffer Publishing Ltd.

4880 Lower Valley Road, Atglen, Pennsylvania 19310

Schiffer Books are available at special discounts for bulk purchases for sales promotions or premiums. Special editions, including personalized covers, corporate imprints, and excerpts can be created in large quantities for special needs. For more information contact the publisher:

Published by Schiffer Publishing Ltd.
4880 Lower Valley Road
Atglen, PA 19310
Phone: (610) 593-1777;
Fax: (610) 593-2002
E-mail: Info@schifferbooks.com

For the largest selection of fine reference books on this and related subjects, please visit our website at:
www.schifferbooks.com
We are always looking for people to write books on new and related subjects. If you have an idea for a book please contact us at the above address.

This book may be purchased from the publisher. Include $5.00 for shipping. Please try your bookstore first. You may write for a free catalog.

In Europe, Schiffer books are distributed by
Bushwood Books
6 Marksbury Ave.
Kew Gardens
Surrey TW9 4JF England
Phone: 44 (0) 20 8392 8585; Fax: 44 (0) 20 8392 9876
E-mail: info@bushwoodbooks.co.uk
Website: www.bushwoodbooks.co.uk

Dedication

Dedicated to my wife Nancy-Ann,
who has put up with the insanity of living
with a crazy man who talks to the dead.
It is only through your love that
I have survived it this far.

Acknowledgments

A special thank you must first be given to two very important people without whose help I would not have ever considered a project like this. First, thanks to my little sister, Marla Brooks, who gave me constant advice and encouragement about the who, what, where, and whys of book writing. Secondly, I must say thank you to Mason Winfield, a good friend and folklorist, who earlier gave me a chance to co-author a book with him, as well as helping me realize that even a dyslexic kid like me could write and follow his dreams.

Next, I would like to thank the following who shared their experiences and opened their buildings to me. Carmen Coleman, John Koerner and Rob Lockhart of Haunted History Tours, The Cheektowaga Historical Society, The North Tonawanda Historical Society, Old Fort Niagara State Park, Geoff Harding, Greg Hoffman, Jeff Kerl, Ryan Willard, John Crocitto, Sandra Barnes, Glenn White, Michelle White, Jena Whitking, Lee Prosser, Ron Nagy, The Lily Dale Historical Museum, David and Tommy Jones, The Para-X Radio Network, all of the fans of *The Black Cat Lounge Radio Hour* and, of course, Dinah Roseberry and Schiffer Books.

Thank You One And All!

Contents

Foreword by Marla Brooks 8

Introduction 10

Chapter 1: Walking the Razor's Edge 12

Chapter 2: The Séance and Talk of Evil 21

Chapter 3: Starting at the End of the Line 30

Chapter 4: Specters of a Forgotten War 44

Chapter 5: A Place Of Life, A Place Of Death 56

Chapter 6: Seneca Witchcraft And Christian Pioneers 70

Chapter 7: Buffalo's Infected District 79

Chapter 8: Of Grease Paint and Broken Dreams 85

Chapter 9: Forgotten Tunnels, Ghosts, and The Town
Ball Room 97

Chapter 10: The Specter Of Death And The Angels of Mercy 102

Chapter 11: Iron Rails and Not So Silent Spirits 108

Chapter 12: The Keepers Of Memories 124

Chapter 13: Places Of Healing 147

Chapter 14: The Vanishing Hitchhiker Of Sugar Road 163

Chapter 15: Spooks About Town And Other Sites Of
Macabre Interest.. 167

Chapter 16: Those Who Spoke To The Dead 180

Bibliography 187

Foreword
by Marla Brooks

When I think of Buffalo, New York, two of my favorite things come to mind. Chicken wings and the Reverend Tim Shaw.

Yummy food and good friends not withstanding, Buffalo is a historical city that originated around 1789 as a small trading community and has grown to be the second most populous city in the state of New York, second only to New York City. The thing about that bit of information is, they are referring to the *living* population, and believe me, there are many more inhabitants in Buffalo and its suburbs than meets the naked eye. In his capacity as both historian and an ordained spiritualist minister and medium, Reverend Tim knows many of the dearly departed on a first name basis.

From ghosts of the War of 1812 to graveyards and Native American burial mounds to shops, theaters and museums, the spirits are very much alive in Western New York because, as I always say, where there is history, there are ghosts.

While some books merely chronicle hauntings and repeat often-told tales, this is more of a journal of sites rather than a cut and dried accounting. The good Reverend brings his own personal experience and insight into the locations he writes about and boy, does he have insight... even in dark, creepy places like Buffalo's forgotten tunnel system.

Of course, I'm kind of partial to the chapter on Seneca Witchcraft, but what can I say? What respectable witch wouldn't be?

And would any book on ghosts and hauntings be worth its salt without a vanishing hitchhiker or a spectre of death?

Reverend Tim's chapter on "Father Baker's Our Lady of Victory" was of particular interest to me. The church and orphanage is a charity that I have supported for many years. Psychic to the Stars, Kenny Kingston, first told me about it, and when I learned the story about Father Nelson Baker, his work and his legacy, I felt that it was one of the worthiest causes I could get involved with.

One day, Tim inadvertently mentioned Father Baker and Our Lady of Victory and was quite surprised that I even knew who Father Baker was with me being on the West Coast and all. When he told me that Father Baker's spirit still walks the halls of the sanctuary he built out of love, his many reported sightings made perfect sense because love conquers all, even to the extent of crossing back from the other side on a regular basis to keep an eye on things.

There are so many haunted locations written about in the book that I got the impression that the ghosts far outnumbered the living; and that's not even counting the millions of chickens who made the ultimate sacrifice to make Buffalo a Foodie Paradise. In reality, it all does come down to food, and don't blame me for the hunger pangs. This book offers up food for thought, nourishment for the soul, and a hunger to read more. So, turn to the next page and dig right in!

~ Marla Brooks
Author of the *Ghosts of Hollywood* series

Introduction

The macabre stories of the Nickle City are sometimes buried just below the surface. All that one needs to do is to scratch the dirt to find that the city of Buffalo, New York, is ripe with instances of ghostly visitations, witchcraft, and hidden worlds. Some say it is the rushing water of the mighty Niagara River that causes this area to be a magnet for unusual sightings and activities. Others feel that it may have been the rich Native American heritage of this highly contested region that has left a bloody imprint upon the land.

Buffalo's very existence was tested by fire during the tragic War of 1812. The village of that era became a smoking ruin that scarred the land for many generations. A hard scrapple life at best, Buffalonians returned after the bloody battle to rebuild their lives. These intrepid souls pressed on and built upon the very graves of their predecessors breathing a new life into the region.

Many of those who have been gifted with psychic awareness feel that Buffalo not only possesses the spirits of the ancient ones, but also those of the industrial age. The importance of its port can never be diminished as well as the fact that the Erie Canal's western terminus was located along her shores. Immigrants who manned the grain mills, warehouses, and sugar refineries filled the streets causing the city to literally burst at its seams and its new gentry were forced to look for new locations upon which to build their mansions. All this activity surely left behind vibratory fields that are still resonating to this very day.

As in all paranormally active regions, there are usually found an undercurrent of unsavory characters as well as instances of naturally occurring epidemics along with the usual murder and mayhem. For the occult enthusiast this is a place that has it all.

There is no one special key to the mystery of why Buffalo is so haunted. We who live here accept the fact that we may never be alone. The voices of past are still heard mixed with the gentle summer breeze if one truly wants to hear them. For those who live there it matters little why spirits may walk in Buffalo but it is the fact that they do.

~Tim Shaw

Chapter 1

Walking the Razor's Edge

Can Science and Belief Co-Exist in Paranormal Research?

In many paranormal circles, there are certain biases towards some metaphysical methodologies and philosophies. While this is necessary in order to build an organized base for research, many in the field tend to be of the "all or nothing" mindset. It is this concept that on many levels serves to alienate individuals and organizations, thus feeding into various rivalries and ill will.

From the very beginning of paranormal research we find such difficulties. The investigations of the post-Victorian age are filled with such testimonials. Admittedly, it has been recorded that there were far more frauds than authentic manifestations of true mental or physical phenomena. This is where science did the modern investigator a service (as well as those of us who believe that the paranormal is part of our own spirituality). It was they who exposed the charlatans who masqueraded as channels for spirit communication. Unfortunately, while this may have been a blow to the "true believers," it did provide serious research that is still in use today.

Currently, in many venues we now experience something that has been festering for many years. The "cult of skepticism" has taken up the vanguard against those who wish to delude the public for whatever the reason. Some in the religious communities many find these skeptics unpalatable, however it is these individuals who are a necessary part of the checks and balances that make up the paranormal investigative community. It is they who set the boundaries for what may be admissible evidence and what is questionable at best. For without boundaries investigators would have no base line to which they might bring their own evidence or experiences for comparison. Thus the "cult of the skeptic" is extremely important to the total undertaking.

On the extreme opposite side of the argument is the "cult of the believer." It is this concept that may have led many of us into the field of paranormal research in the first place. It also provides the spiritual or religious base that is necessary to support the individual belief system. However, adherents may take the dogma of that belief system as omnipotent, critically limiting their own investigations by simply taking whatever happens as a paranormal event without examining any factors associated with the occurrence. Blind belief is therefore more dangerous than anything that science has ever created in the laboratory and severely limits the investigator.

Within the study of the paranormal, a "mid level" must be attained. As we know, the paranormal does not respond to the checks and balances of strict scientific methodology. Thus there must be a level of belief associated with its demonstrations and recorded observation. Likewise there must be a verification process through which recorded evidence of a paranormal occurrence is categorized and examined. One concept is seemingly intertwined with the other.

Paranormal investigators must comb through the files of those whom have previously undertaken research into this topic. They must follow up the leads needed to open the path of truth no matter how unorthodox they may at the moment seem to them. Likewise investigators must also be willing to submit evidence collected for examination and comment without hesitation. These conclusions must be accepted with grace and dignity, to which they are then applied as new baseline for your upcoming investigations.

Investigators must learn to accept what is scientifically sound, question what is unexplained, be truthful in our observations, and finally share with others these experiences. Without skepticism, belief, scientific methodology, and communication within the field there will be no advances in this discipline.

The Basic Tools of the Trade

There are many tools that are utilized by both the Paranormal Investigator, as well as those who commune with the spirits. It is important to understand that whatever tool being used during an investigation, the investigator is ultimately the deciding factor on whether it is successful or not. So remember the old adage: "Practice Makes Perfect." The more you work with any tool, the more receptive and skilled you become. Also, as you may notice, I am not advocating the use of a lot of high-tech gear. I feel that you can get great results with inexpensive or homemade equipment. Of course the best tool in your kit is your own common sense.

Here are a few of the gadgets that I use on investigations:

Digital Recorder

Any digital recorder will suffice for most types of paranormal investigations. I recommend that you use one with a variable speed playback option that is featured for transcription work. By altering the audio playback speed you may hear words and phrases that are sometimes not within our linguistic cadence. Analog recorders that require a micro cassette are also good to use but do not usually come with the necessary adapters to easily upload into your computer for analysis.

Digital Camera

One of the true marvels of the modern age, the digital camera has revolutionized paranormal investigations. Digital cameras produce instantaneous feedback, are cheaper to use, and are more sensitive to infrared and ultraviolet light. The downside is that they do not produce a negative and the quality of the photograph is not as good as when using most films. The light from whatever you are photographing "hits" an electric mechanism called a "Charged Coupled Device." It is this unit that interprets the electrons of light as "pre-programmed colors." What this simply means is that the image is not a direct impression of the subject in the same way as it occurs on a negative. Some investigators believe that because a spirit is an entity attempting to utilize electromagnetic frequencies, digital cameras are more sensitive to interpreting this type of energy form. However, it must be remembered that all light does contain the capacity for electrical impulses, but not all of these impulses will produce light. The "CCD" in some cases will interpret a charge that does not produce light and is invisible to the eye creating a false image or effect.

Infrared Illuminators

This is an external device that enhances the capacity to take photographs in the dark without illuminating space with bright white light. They work exactly like your human eyes except are more sensitive to infrared instead of the visible spectrum.

Electromagnetic Field Meter (EMF)

These units are relatively inexpensive and are designed to detect naturally occurring disruptions in magnetic fields. Originally designed to pick up radiation leakage from cell phones and microwave ovens, EMF meters are extremely useful when doing an initial location "walk through" pinpointing areas of high EMF. Prolonged exposure may lead to skin rashes, hallucinations, and in extreme cases cancer. It is also believed that ghosts can manipulate EMF in order to manifest, affect physical objects or communicate with us. The theory is that the closer an entity may come to an EMF meter, the higher the reading, thus by their movement, they can give *yes or no* answers by producing such spikes.

Motion Detectors

These small alarms will sound when movement is detected. Devices such as these are used primarily to monitor for human movement at a location and the tampering of target objects.

Dowsing Rods

When using dowsing "L" rods, the rods will demonstrate a reaction when they come in contact with locations of increased energy levels. The "intent" for which the dowsing rods are used is most important – otherwise you may be getting a reaction every time you get near water pipes or electric lines. Dowsing rods can also detect spirit energy and can be used for spirit communication once *yes and no* reactions are established.

Pendulum

A form of dowsing and divination, the pendulum is simply a light weight suspended from a string or cord. It will begin to circle once suspended, when EMF or spirit energy is present. While this is a tool that can be used for spirit communication, some feel that this may be psychokinetic or have a subconscious origin.

Shot Glass

No, this is not for those investigations where you need to get your courage up. A shot glass can be simply used as a planchette in spirit communication. This can be used either with an alphabet board or without (similar to spirit boards).

Target Objects

These are items that may "tempt" the spirit into manipulating them. For example, a stuffed animal may be used when attempting to validate the existence of a child's spirit. The object is set up in a certain manner, photographed, or a chalk outline is drawn around it to gage any movement. Also objects may be placed in an "observation box" or frame. This is an enclosure with a clear window, such as an upside down aquarium where items placed within can be easily seen but cannot be easily tampered with. An example would be dice set with certain numbers showing or a pencil or a small pad.

Thermometer

Both digital and ordinary thermometers can be used to check for any changes in the location's temperature. Spirits will sometimes use the energy within an enclosed space to manifest phenomena thus creating a chill or a cold spot. While effective, you must be aware of anything that will allow a breeze into the environment which will affect the ambient temperature.

Flashlight

Originally brought along as an illuminator, we now find that "twist lens" styles, such as manufactured by the "Maglite" corporation, can be used in spirit communication. The on and off switch responds to the twisting motion of the lens housing. By positioning the housing to where the light will almost go on with a slight downward pressure on the lens it is thought that a spirit may be able to exert that slight pressure enabling communication.

Paranormal Encounters

In order to be an effective investigator, one needs to understand that hauntings and ghosts fall in to several basic classifications. The following is meant to be a general guide to what maybe encountered when exploring the paranormal realm.

Hauntings

Traditional or Intelligent Haunting

This is when a spirit attempts to manifest into the physical plane and interact with people through the use of mental or physical phenomena. In this type of haunting there must be some form of "real time" direct interaction or meaningful communication taking place.

Residual Haunting

This is where an energy imprint has taken root in the earthly atmosphere. Locations become storage batteries and this absorbed energy replays a scene over and over again. In this type of haunting, ghostly manifestations, smells, and sounds are present but will not interact with people. When approached or confronted, these apparitions will normally vanish. Windows and doors may open and close, however, it is normally just the expansion of already existing energy. Atmospheric conditions can play an important role in residual hauntings. There maybe a correlation between higher levels of static electricity or barometric pressure and residual activity.

Portals and Vortexes

Basically, a portal is believed to be a doorway to another dimension. Cemeteries have been thought to be prime locations, however, these openings can be found almost anywhere. The theory is that spirits, demons, or even aliens, may use these doorways to cross over from one sphere to another.

Types of Ghosts

Visiting Spirit Personalities

These are entities that literally come to the earth plane to visit, check on loved ones, bring messages, or comfort the living. They are not "attached" to this plane but come here of their own choosing. These types of entities may or may not make their visit outwardly known.

Self Earthbound Spirits

There is a multitude of reasons why a spirit personality will become earth bound. Reasons such as confusion at the time of death, unfinished business, fear of an afterlife retribution, a swift and tragic passing, an intense connection with the physical body or physical location, low self esteem, depression or a down right refusal to leave are but just a few of the viable reasons why a spirit "chooses" to become earth bound. These types of entities can cause paranormal activity and are often confused with poltergeists.

Animal Spirits

These are the spirit forms of departed animals. Most commonly found are beloved pets that humans have developed strong emotional attachments to. However other spirit animals may be encountered at such places that may have held them. Farms and slaughter houses often have animal spirits associated with them. Spirit Animals are also traditionally believed to possess great wisdom and are revered in many traditional earth-based religions and cultures.

Energy Imprints

Often called "Trails" or "Residual Energy," these are paranormal occurrences or ghostly sightings that are not related to interactive spirit personalities. This type of energy repeats itself either on a regular or irregular cycle.

Spirit Attachments

When doing an investigation at any location, there is always a chance that you might bring an entity home with you. The causes for this are many. Some investigators believe that there are usually two distinct reasons in the majority of cases.

1. **Sympathy** – Many times, the spirit personality will actually identify with an emotional attribute of the investigator. This causes a similarity in vibrations, thus the spirit may decide to accompany that "like vibration."

2. **Physical Disturbances** – If an existing vibrational field is "disturbed" to which the spirit personality has attached itself, the spirit may in turn attach to any living being found at the location being investigated. This is especially common in places where remodeling or construction work is taking place.

I have found that the best way to rid one's self of these spirit personalities is to always say a prayer of intent or protection before and after any investigation. I like to include the phrase:

"I wish to leave all spirits here at this location."

This is all part of the concept of spiritual control. If you believe it, so it is.

Addictive Entities

These are entities that, while on the earth, suffered from various chemical and psychological dependencies. They are attracted to those in the living who may share similar traits. In some instances, they can take over the addict's physical body temporarily in order to "physically feel" the effects of whatever their victim's addiction presently is.

Ghostly Mimics

These are entities that can pose as human beings and be visually experienced by the common man. They do this in order to accomplish a goal, sometimes not easily understood from a human perspective.

Non – Human Poltergeists - or "Noisy Ghosts"

This type of phenomena tends to manifest itself in physical ways in order to bring attention to the spirit presence. These cases may last for many years. However, in some cases, poltergeists may not be intelligent spirits at all but simply a form of residual energy that has been triggered by a particular person's vibrations.

Human Poltergeists

This is phenomena that centers on a single person, usually an adolescent girl and normally one that is emotionally troubled. (This phenomenon can also manifest around adolescent boys.) It is sometimes triggered by spirit entities, however recent theories now feel that objects are manipulated through the unconscious use of psychokinetic energy by the victim.

Human-Created Entities

Back in the 1970s, a group of Canadian researchers gathered to test a theory. For this experiment, they "created" a spirit personality by the name of "Phillip." This group went so far as to create an entire history for this entity, communicating with him through the use of table tipping. Once all of the members of the control group began to seriously believe in the essence of Phillip, raps through the table began. Upon asking questions, it was found that the entity purporting to be "Phillip" answered the various questions asked correctly. At one point, the researcher whose home was being used for the experiment, had trouble opening his door and found that the table used in the experiment became lodged against it – with no one being in the residence at the time. "Phillip" ended his communication when one researcher broke ranks and announced to the "sitters" present that "Phillip" was only made up. At that point all communication stopped.

Some mediums believe that spirits are hungry for human contact. This is very common when using table tipping and "talking boards." However, it is now believed that this phenomenon may be triggered by the combined energy of a group focused upon a single topic. Some researchers feel that this is an example of the conscious use of psychokinetic energy.

Elementals

These are considered the spirits of the earth. There are four classes of elementals that are associated with the elements of air, fire, water, and earth. These entities are found in most places and can inhabit practically everything. Several earth- based and aboriginal religions believe that there are spirits inhabiting the rivers, thunder, winds, rocks, clouds, and most natural surroundings. One must be careful when working with elementals as they can become quite nasty and violent when offended. It also should be noted that elementals have never been born or have died.

Deiform Spirits

These entities are various in scope and most often will manifest in the physical forms of deities or godlike beings. They are most often found in the areas that are on or near ancient ruins and burial grounds. It is reported that they can become very violent if insulted or disrespected in any way.

The Demonic Kingdom And Parasitical Spirits

This category will depend entirely upon your own belief system. (The importance is placed on how a negative entity will work within your own belief system). The goal sought by a dark entity is to take control of a victim's body and soul. In most cases of demonic possession, the entity has been openly "invited" into the life of the victim through a ritual or some other form of acceptance. The phases of this type of phenomena are personal infestation, obsession, oppression, depression, and various stages of possession. The end result is the degradation of the human host and death.

Chapter 2

The Séance and Talk of Evil

The Holy Communion Of Spirit Communication

An evening breeze, mildly charged with static electricity announced the coming of a light spring rain. The darkened hall, barely illuminated by flickering candlelight created an atmosphere of macabre beauty. Those guests invited to take part in this sacred communion, were silently ushered into the room. The medium's assistant assigned with the task of seating alternating genders arranged the table in such a way as to have an equal balance of chi energy. When all was in readiness, three knocks rapped upon a door by this helper was the signal for the medium to enter the room. Silently he took his place at the head of the table.

So began a séance that was held in East Aurora, New York, May, 2008.

Many mediums consider the demonstration of séance to be an "intense communion with the Spirit World." It is a special time when the energies of the living can become intertwined with the departed producing physical and mental phenomena such as object levitation, apports, asports, direct and indirect voice, slate writing, transfiguration, apparitions, channeling, as well as spirit to human mind telepathy.

Those who study this form of Spirit interaction have generally acknowledged that there are two categories of "séances." The first is referred to as the "Open Séance" where a medium gathers with different people called "sitters" on each occasion it is held. The second form of séance is called the "Closed Séance." In this style, the same sitters, students, and mediums will gather at the same day of the week, at the same time, and at predetermined regular intervals. In this manner the "sitters" energies will gradually become in-sync with one another's as well creating a PSI energy charged atmosphere which is conducive to the creation of phenomena.

During the late 1800s, séances were elaborate affairs that included certain rituals and the use of "spirit tools." Many rituals were nothing more than saying a simple prayer at the beginning and at the end of the séance. Others included the consumption of a light meal consisting of broth, the white meat of a chicken, and white wine. As servants cleared the table, the sitters would change into light-colored or white clothing. Upon returning to the table, they would begin to sing hymns in order to raise their individual vibrations. Sometimes a "spirit cabinet," which is a wooden frame "box" that was covered with dark cloth, would be used. Here a medium would enter in the hopes of creating a super-charged metaphysical atmosphere. Other times the medium would simply sit in a chair and go into a trance.

For a séance that was held in East Aurora, New York, during 2008, I had been asked to research, develop, as well as conduct a form of this historic practice. I chose to use a few of the aspects of the traditional séance out of respect of my own family members who had also been mediums. However, I wanted to add into the service one or two modern additions. Since candles were taboo in the building where we met, I suggested that small electric tea lights be used in their place. Next, because there were fifteen people who had been invited to attend, two long rectangular tables were pushed together lengthwise, replacing a normal dinner-style round table.

While I have no fear about leading a séance or working in a state of trance, my Spirit Guides during a meditation advised me to work with an assistant, which I now refer to as a "guardian." I asked one of my advanced mediumship unfoldment students to aid me with this endeavor. His duties were not only to explain the "etiquette" of a séance to the sitters, and protect me from any bright light which could prove harmful to me when I went into a trance state, but also to be ready to bring me out of the trance if I was hesitant to return from wherever it is that I go when I allow my body to be controlled by Spirit.

Our séance began with an explanation of why séances were held, the type that we would be conducting that evening, as well as the traditional tools used. These tools consisted of a Spirit Trumpet, a small bell, a candle, and a set of banded writing slates with chalk.

I opened the service with a prayer of protection and asked the Infinite Intelligence of the Universe to bring close all of our departed family members, friends, guides, and teachers. Next, I instituted "boundaries," requesting that only the "highest and best" of the Spirit World work through us during this demonstration. After the prayer, a silent meditation was held followed by the singing of the first stanza of "Amazing Grace." Then I politely asked Spirit to give us a sign of

Séance Spirit Trumpets.

its presence. It was at this time when I first began to hear the table in front of me creak. Sitters nearby felt the table pulsate with energy which is quite common during the séance experience. Upon hearing the sound, I lifted my hands in order to prove to the others sitters that the creaking which emanated from below their hands was not being produced by me. This sound continued throughout most of the séance.

Slowly, I slipped into a trance and I am told that I channeled a rather forceful gentleman who enjoyed referring to us humans as spirits contained within "coffins of flesh." Several "sitters" have told me that the spirit related a story about how many of us seem to miss the importance of having and appreciating life. People walk around this earth missing all of the beauty that our world has to offer. When this spectral orator had finished his message I was ushered back to this "plane" by my Guide. Immediately I wondered why my right hand ached and was later told that I had been banging it on the table as the orator had emphasized certain important remarks.

Once this entity left my body, I felt the need to give Spirit Greetings and Messages, but quickly tired after relating only a few. Spirit instructed me to ask my assistant to bring forth any messages that he might have been holding, which he gladly did.

Gradually, I could sense that the energy in the room, which had originally been quite elevated, was beginning to wane. It had been approximately forty-five minutes and I felt that it was time for the séance to end. A prayer of thanks was said, as well as one of healing for the world and our friends who may have fallen ill. I thanked everyone for their attendance and left the table, going into a room by myself in order to ground, pray, and rejuvenate.

This demonstration of séance is the culmination of the many paranormal experiences that I have witnessed over the years. All of my studies have served to convince me that a revival of the traditional practices of Spiritualism should be attempted as there is a need great need for Spirit interaction.

While the practice of séance is a wonderful tool, I highly suggest that people interested in holding or leading one receive proper training from a qualified teacher. This is not a Victorian parlor game. Séance has been and will remain a very serious business.

Séance Writing Slates.

The Dark Night of Spirit

"How are you fallen from Heaven, Lucifer! Son of the Dawn! Cut down to the ground! And once you dominated the peoples!"
~Isaiah 14:12 – 19

Was it your interest in the occult that convinced you to watch the cult movie classic, *The Exorcist*? Who amongst us could ever forget those horrible scenes of a young child tortured by demonic forces? We now know that the inspiration for the original novel and subsequent film was based upon an actual case of an exorcism that took place in 1949. Was it merely just an account of an isolated occurrence or was it perhaps the harbinger of something far more sinister?

In my work as a medium and paranormal investigator, I know that true possessions by a negative or demonic entity are rare. Yet according to colleagues who are actual exorcists, modern claims of demonic attacks seem to be on the rise across the world.

For this chapter I must stress that I am concentrating only upon the actual acts of possession and not the many forms of mental illnesses that can mimic it. (This is why it is so important that a person who may believe that they are in a state of possession have a comprehensive medical and psychiatric evaluation before actually pursuing an actual exorcism.) If demonic activity is suspected, I suggest that proper professionals be immediately contacted. Also, at this time, another warning should be issued. There are many in the metaphysical and paranormal fields who claim to be "demonologists." Most have only a passing degree of education or competency in the field and can cause more harm than good. A true demonologist is a person who is either a member of the clergy assigned to those duties or a person who has an association with such an expert, possesses a great deal of knowledge, and experience working closely with an exorcist. The demonic is something not to be taken lightly!

Thus stated, let us examine human possession. It appears in two forms: full and transient.

Full Possession

In a full possession (such as was shown in the aforementioned movie), the demonic entity will take full-time control of the body of the victim. Also the victim will exhibit strength beyond that of a normal human being, may speak in foreign or unknown languages, putrid smells will be noticed by witnesses, rapping sounds on walls (usually in threes to mock the trinity if the victim is of a Christian religion), religious items will be broken or disappear, and audible growling sounds are sometimes heard (the demonic is seldom captured through electronic voice phenomena I have been told). Often suspected victims will demonstrate drastic personality changes, use foul language, experience changes in the pitch of their voices, have writing or symbols appear on their skin, begin to bite or scratch others, stare without blinking such as in a catatonic state (dilated pupils to the point where the white areas of the eyes are absent), cause heavy objects and furniture to levitate, as well as producing multiple unknown voices. Investigators have witnessed the creation of bile-like substances and victims are examined for various signs of sexual attack. (For the purposes of this chapter, I have only included a few of the characteristics of possession, as I do not wish anyone to self diagnose themselves as possessed. However, these are the most common.) The victim will also have a long history of external or poltergeist activity associated directly to themselves that have been witnessed by others.

Transient Possession

In a transient possession, the entity will show most of the already mentioned phenomenon; however it will come and go from the victim as it pleases. The next question is: "How does one become possessed?" That is a theory as varied as the individuals who become afflicted, and each case is different. Most demonologists believe that the victim must allow in some manner the entity access to their physical body. A common example can be someone who uses any form of indiscriminate divination, allowing the negative entity to deceive them into thinking that they are a dead relative or friend who "needs" to accomplish a task or bring through absolute spiritual communication. Other times "soul victims" (people described as those being "pure of heart" and considered challenges to the demonic world) are tormented. Another avenue of deception is one found in many classic stories, such as the person who sells his soul to the devil for an earthly favor or reward. Regardless of the method of entry, the bottom line is that the demonic hates the human race and its goal is to debase and take control of the life of individual until such a time that the victim is reduced to an animal-like state or succumbs to death.

Many religions do not believe that the devil exists. They feel that there are negative spirits or entities that may be earthbound, and for some reason, attempt to torment the victim for their own well being. Addictive spirits will sometimes fall into that category. Other times, entities wish to feed off of the emotions that fear and confusion will bring which are created within the mind of the victim. Whether it is a demon or negative entity, to the person experiencing this form of manipulation, it is traumatizing.

The stages of possession are actually quite straight forward and documented in many western societies. It begins with "infestation." That is the time when the demonic slowly creeps into the life of the victim. Usually, this takes the form of phenomena that is commonly associated with hauntings. Cold spots, shadow beings, and most of the other trappings of the paranormal world made famous by modern television shows can be present in such cases. Also paranormal investigators and mediums over the years all agree that spirit activity can occur at almost anytime of the day or night. It should be noted that demonic activity is most common when natural light is absent, thus nighttime is when activity may peak.

There is currently a controversial theory that the victim can become "obsessed" with doing something that is linked to the paranormal. There are modern cases where victims have begun to work with the various tools of paranormal investigations, such as digital voice recorders used in the collection of EVPs. The evidence captured may start off innocently enough, but will eventually become threatening and obscene. Even when this happens, some people will not stop. Several demonologists believe that this may be the opening needed by a lesser or negative spirit for a demonic entity to enter into the life of the victim.

The next stage of possession is that of "oppression." This is a stage where intense physical and psychological attack begins, whereby the entity seeks to control a person's thoughts for a time. Again, the attacks are all coordinated to break the will of the victim, much like many interrogation techniques that can make a person so desperate for the treatment to stop that they will admit their participation in a certain crime or activity whether they are guilty or not. In many cases, the victim will begin to suffer from depression, paranoia, as well as sleeping and eating disorders. The victim will hear demonic voices oftentimes giving them instructions on how to conduct their lives – usually to their detriment. The ability to ask for outside or religious help is also greatly hindered by threats of punishment by the entities seeking control.

The last stage is of course the actual "possession." True "possession," regardless of modern claims, is actually quite rare, but not totally hidden from view . With the rise of the popularity of paranormal programming, I have personally seen a jump in requests for investigating alleged demonic infestations and attacks.

"Attachments" are often a common problem faced by those who do not possess a strong belief system or use spiritual protection. All holistic practitioners as well as paranormal investigators should take the subject of negative or demonic entities, along with addictive spirits, quite seriously. It is not unheard of for well-meaning people to attract or suffer a "spiritual or spirit attachment" after performing a procedure on a client. Likewise, paranormal investigators run these risks just by the fact that they are often at a location where an entity of this nature may have been reported.

"Targeting" is another danger, one that I have personally experienced. This form of "infestation" takes place when a negative entity feels that a person may be a threat to its purpose. This entity will do what it can to scare or oppress that person until they give up their desire to help the victim. Also, if that cannot be accomplished, the entity may "target" the family or friends of such a Samaritan.

In the fall of 2007, I was asked to consult on a case of possible poltergeist/incubus activity. After doing the initial telephone interviews, I began to experience phenomena at my home that was inconsistent with the normal spirit activity present there. I personally was awoken at 3:33am for almost a week straight (remember that 3's are a mock of the trinity and negative activity is associated with darkness). I heard footsteps and dragging sounds in my home, my decision and judgment-making processes began to be affected, I suffered from symptoms of depression, gave up my reading practice, stopped attending religious services, and experienced personality changes that friends readily spoke to me about. Upon finally realizing what was happening, I told whatever it was that I knew of its presence and demanded that it leave me in peace. I next performed several Reiki healings on myself and stepped away from the case – after consulting with people whom I knew were better suited to aid the family in question. Immediately, after ending my involvement in the case, all infestation ceased and I felt normal again.

So does possession actually exist? I believe so. Is Satan or the devil the true cause of possession? Personally, I do not believe that to be true. However, I will say that in my experience, our universe is one made to be of balance. As such I believe that there is a source for ultimate good. If this is true, then there must also be a source for evil that lurks in the shadows.

Will you ever be exposed to such an evil? I pray that you never are.

Chapter 3
Starting At The End Of The Zine

Haunted Graveyards, Lost Souls, And Roving Bones

Do the dead really rest in peace? Shall our bones stay where they lay once our loved ones have passed onto the spectral side? This is of course a question that we shall have to wait for an answer until such a time when we breathe no more. In our modern society, it is taken for granted that when our earthly remains have been committed to the ground that they shall linger there undisturbed. Unfortunately for many, this is not always the case.

Places of burial are considered consecrated or holy ground by most cultures. More often then not we find incidences of cemeteries that have been moved in order to meet the needs of man. A new rail spur that rips through a traditional Native American burial mound, roadway construction that literally grinds bones into its foundations, the need for more farmlands, industrial parks, and living space are more common than many of us realize.

The city of Buffalo is no different than any other metropolis of its size. Time after time we see examples of Native American burial grounds that have been moved, forgotten, or in many cases just "plowed into the sod." Even white cemeteries have suffered similar fates.

Many of these former resting places have reported spectral phenomena while others may simply be waiting for the right person to awaken the spirits who slumber there. The following is but a sampling of the roving cemeteries and burial sites of Western New York. Remember to tread softly when you visit these places.

Native American Sites
The Old Buffum Street Burial Grounds

Original Sign From Burial Ground.

Formerly located on Buffum Street in the South Buffalo District, this burial ground was once a part of the former Buffalo Creek Indian Reservation. When observing this area, you can easily notice what has been traditionally held as a weathered burial mound, perhaps the last within the City of Buffalo's limits. Before 1639, the area was occupied by the Wenro bands and after the 1780s, the Seneca Nation. Excavations at the site have revealed a rich assortment of stone and bone implements.

Following the American Revolution, many Seneca's were forced to leave their ancestral homes in the Genesee Valley for inclusion on government -mandated reservations. As this area was already considered a place of burial, it was reused for newer internments. It was in this Native American cemetery that such notables as the great Seneca orator Red Jacket and the "White Woman of the Genesee," Mary Jemison, were originally interred. Once the reservation lands were sold, the cemetery was closed and many of the remains exhumed and sent to Forest Lawn Cemetery for reburial.

Buffum Street Cemetery.

During the summer of 2009, I visited the site in order to do an early morning, passive paranormal investigation. On advice of medicine man Willie "Windwalker" Gibson, I offered a "gift" of tobacco to the ancestors and to the Great Spirit before starting. Using only a voice recorder, I asked several questions and found, upon my review of the evidence, that I did in fact capture what sounded like a very faint rhythmic chanting.

There has been paranormal activity reported in several of the homes that surround what is left of the burial mound. Also there are various reports of electrical anomalies that occur within the houses, ghostly chanting, unexplained sounds, and objects within these homes moving. Perhaps it is the restless spirits of those whom have been relocated, back to look for their bones. Or could it be that many Native American bodies still repose under the streets, rose bushes, and well manicured lawns?

Fenton Street

As often found in the pursuit of progress, there is an occasional darker side to this endeavor. The Fenton Street Native American burial site was destroyed when it was deemed necessary for the land to be graded during the construction of Barnard Street. When work began, it is said that seventy-five sets of remains were discovered and later reburied in a "Potter's Field." It is a strong possibility that other remains not found became part of the newly graded street. Is it no wonder that our Native brothers cannot rest in peace?

Edge of Neolithic Burial Mound.

Armine Near Seneca Street

This once-large burial mound has now been totally obliterated by private homes. Anthropologists believe that it may have been part of the old Buffum Street Indian village.

Forest Lawn Cemetery

This is *the* burial ground in that has become the final resting place for anyone who was someone in Western New York. Pioneers, soldiers, merchants, bankers, artists, writers, and even President Millard Fillmore lie in repose under sometimes extravagant memorials of stone. However, before the coming of the European, it is said to be the site of a fierce battle between the Iroquois Confederacy and the Neutral Nation (Kahquas). Those killed in this battle were buried in a mass burial, presumably a mound. Unfortunately, the location of the battle, as well as the burial, can only be speculated upon, but if true, those remains still stay resting in consecrated grounds.

Lost Native American burial sites have also been located in neighboring Western New York Communities.

Forest Lawn Cemetery.

West Seneca, New York
Potter Road

Located near the Buffum Street burial grounds is a high flat area along Cazenovia Creek. Skeletal remains have been found which contained both stone tools as well as early European trade goods.

Potter Road, Corner of Reiser

There is research that suggests several cabins were built by members of the Onondaga tribe. When the land was being cleared for redevelopment burial sites were found with various mortuary offerings which included silver broaches.

Cheektowaga, New York

The town of Cheektowaga, New York, originally named by the Seneca as Ji-ik-do-wa-gah which means "place of the crabapple," has at least one Native American burial site.

William Street
(Where it Crosses Cayuga Creek)

After the Revolutionary War, Cayuga refugees built cabins and established a small community around 1780. Town historians believe their burial ground was located near the banks of Cayuga Creek. An archeological dig conducted on Cayuga Road at the site of a present-day retirement facility reveals evidence of stone tool-making technology. Could this also been the site of the reported burial ground? Homeowners have reported strange lights that have been seen near the creek. Also some experience an "uneasy feeling" or of being "watched" when walking in the woods behind the retirement home.

Early European and Military Burial Grounds
Corner of Exchange and Washington

This may be the location of the first European Graveyard in the area now known as Buffalo, New York. When digging a cellar in the early 1870s, workers unearthed several skeletons that were believed to some of the areas earliest settlers.

The Grave of Seneca Orator, Red Jacket.

Franklin Square

The old Erie County Hall building is located on top of grounds that belonged to an early cemetery which contained the graves of both settlers as well as soldiers from the War of 1812. When talking with county employees, there have been whispered stories told of a ghostly woman and man seen strolling down several hallways.

The Cold Spring Burial Grounds

This cemetery was located on the corner of Delaware and Ferry Streets and saw to the interment of both rural families as well as the War of 1812 hero, Job Hoysington. The building that is now located on the site was originally known as the Conner's house and is currently the home of Gilda's Club of Western New York, a residence for cancer patients receiving treatment and their families. When Ferry Street was widened in the 1870s, many human bones were discovered and eventually exhumed for reburial in Forest Lawn Cemetery.

The Black Rock Burial Grounds

Once bordered by Pennsylvania, Jersey, and Fourteenth Streets, this burial ground was originally used as a "Potter's Field" by the almshouse that was located nearby during the 1820s.

Karpels Manuscript Museum.

With the ever increasing need for private housing, many of the gravesites were relocated to Forest Lawn Cemetery. Later, during improvements made to Rogers and Circle Streets, bones were discovered and thought

to be from this cemetery. In 2005, a local paranormal investigative group was called to check out a nearby private residence where they discovered human bones on display in the house. They were told that the bones were actually found when digging in the garden. Could these remains have been from one or more of the unmarked poor?

Delaware and Church Streets

This was the site of a temporary military field hospital active during War of 1812. When road improvements were made, construction workers uncovered skeletal remains and what was left of a coffin. Artifacts found with the burial reveal that its occupant was a military Army Lieutenant.

East North Street

Buffalo's City Honors School has the distinction of being built on the site of a burial ground necessitated by an epidemic. During a $40 million dollar renovation project, seventy-five burials were found and it is estimated that at least twice that number may have been buried there. It was established in 1832 during what is thought to have been a cholera outbreak. In 1885, when the area became "Masten Park," many of the remains were then moved to Forest Lawn. However with the discovery of an infant and three adults in December of 2007, it was determined that more graves were indeed still on the property. Also when excavated, extensive grave desecration was found as it seems that grave robbers dug up fresh burials in order to plunder the dead of their valuables. In addition, it was found that they took skulls and large bones (probably sale to medical colleges and to physicians), leaving the smaller ones behind.

The Sweeney Family Burial Grounds

This family burial ground located on Payne Avenue in the City of North Tonawanda was probably first established in 1825 after the building of the Erie Canal. The property was originally owned by James Sweeney and was located on his farm. Although it is felt that there were earlier burials, the first recorded ones took place in 1837. It was officially declared a cemetery when surveyor Tobias Witmer drew it on one of the first area maps in 1857 and was later incorporated in 1868 as the Colonel John Sweeny Rural Cemetery, Inc. Of the notables that reside within its embrace is Allen Herschel, who in 1901, formed a company that carved some of the most beautiful and sought after carousel animals in the world.

The Root Woman Called Black Hannah

In this peaceful cemetery, those of lesser fame are buried. One such person interred there is Hannah Johnson, better known as the escaped slave, "Black Hannah." She passed from this world on June 22, 1883, and was buried in an unmarked grave.

Hannah Johnson traveled to freedom along the route of the Underground Railroad. The rustic cabin in which she lived for over forty years was located on the old Basenberg Farm, north of Sweeney Street. On this property a magical sulfur well, whose water possessed great healing qualities, was located. News of this spread throughout the state and people from many walks of life would venture to her humble home in order to partake of this miracle water cure.

Sweeney Family Cemetery.

In the 1800s, flower and herbal remedies were the mainstay of the medical profession's arsenal. It seems probable that Hannah may have also been an herbalist or what is called a "root worker" in the religion of Voodoo. She was said to have grown some of the areas most beautiful flowers. In fact, Alice Hiestand wrote in 1965 that she [Hannah] must have had "a yen for flowers and cultivated some around her cabin. Long after the cabin disappeared, garden flowers grew wild around the cabin site and were found even as late as the 30s or 40s."

According to her obituary, she was said to be a "fortune teller." People who knew her recalled that Hannah's favorite form of divination was the reading of tea leaves. There is a story that was told about a young man who sought her out to receive some insights as to his upcoming affairs. Hannah stared intently at the symbols made by the rapidly drying tea leaves in his cup. Slowing lifting her head, then looking him in the eyes, she uttered: "I have nothing to tell you." How prophetic was that reading you may ask? Soon afterwards on a trip to Buffalo, he disappeared without a trace.

While the question of her current ghostly presence in the Sweeney Family Burial Grounds is questioned, we do know that the spirit of Hannah Johnson is still with us all. Each time that we look at a beautiful wild flower we shall know that Hannah is there. It is she who lovingly tends to these plants in death as she did in life.

The Specters of 1920

Among the many stories recounted by the life-long residents of North Tonawanda, there is one that remains intriguing to this day. It concerns the frightening appearance of several ghostly apparitions who made themselves known in 1920.

At a home on Bryant Street, which is located directly behind the old Sweeney Family Burial Grounds, Anthony Ross was sleeping peacefully in his bedroom. Suddenly he was aroused from his slumber by a gust of cool air and having his blankets pulled from his bed. Being rendered mute, he watched in horror as the "form of a woman slid into his room through a window." He described this wandering ghost as taking very short, "childlike steps" towards him before vanishing into thin air. Understandably, he was quite unnerved by this experience and moved his family to the Washington Hotel, offering the keys to his house to anyone who wished to stay there. A brave youth took up the challenge and went into the home the very next night. It was reported that he experienced some sort of paranormal phenomena, however the encounter left the poor kid paralyzed with fright.

After a few quiet months, another spectral visitor made its presence known in the area. On June 11th, a seven-foot spirit materialized dressed in white robes and floated past the former Felton Street Grammar School, which was also located on Bryant Street. This time the ghost was witnessed by several motorists including Fred C. Sprenger, a policeman. All were stopped dead in their tracks by the sight of this entity.

Members of the Eldredge Bicycle Club swore that they would patrol the area and if the ghost appeared, they would chase it wherever it would lead them. An old saying within Spiritualist circles says, "Be careful what you wish for, for you may surely get it." One night, another spirit appeared near the cemetery; this time in the guise of a Native American, complete with long, flowing hair, ceremonial feathers, and possessing an abnormally large head, hands, but lacking feet. As this ghost floated off, the members of the club leapt upon their bicycles and chased the specter until it stopped. The brave bicyclists surrounded it, but the "Indian" seemed to just "slip away." However this time the apparition that they chased had somehow morphed into the outline of a skeleton that was covered with a white robe.

When news of the ghostly happenings reached Buffalo, a Spiritualist group traveled to the cemetery. After holding was is rumored to have been a séance of sorts, they declared that the ghost was that of Mr. Norman Shear who had been murdered the previous September along Ensminger Road. However that answer only satisfied a few residents.

Another Spiritualist Society was brought in to investigate and its president announced that they now had the real reason as to why these hauntings were occurring. An election was being held to decide if Tonawanda and North Tonawanda should be consolidated. It was discovered through spirit communication that the entity responsible for all of the strange occurrences was in fact the ghost of a man who came back to oversee the election. The people of North Tonawanda, weary of months of guarding cemeteries and chasing ghosts through school yards, seemed to just accept that explanation. Apparently the ghost did not wish the consolidation to take place and after it was voted down was not heard from again.

We may never know why the spirits became so restless in 1920. Be it because of local politics, murder, or any other number of reasons that year was remembered as a time of excitement and curiosity by all who experienced it.

There are long-standing traditions in both Native American and European cultures that the spirits of the departed do not rest when their burials are disturbed. Could this account for some of the paranormal phenomena that takes place near these former burial grounds?

Could it be that the wandering spirits that are often seen or felt at these locations are really looking for their earthly remains, or is it just the residual vibrations of those whose outer shells were sent to the grounds of these lost burial grounds? Perhaps we shall never know.

Chapter 4

Specters of a Forgotten War

Buffalo and the War of 1812

The bloody War of 1812 began as a challenge to the sovereignty of the fledgling United States government. Years earlier, a ragtag army was transformed into a trained and disciplined military force that had won independence for thirteen struggling colonies. Now this army would once again be needed to answer the call to arms. The war, which lasted from 1812 to 1815, erupted over stringent international trade restrictions, the impressments of American sailors while on the high seas, as well as the arming of Native American warriors during this nations western expansion by its former master, Great Britain. This would become a war that would leave a jagged scar upon the landscape of Western New York for generations to come.

The Theater of Operations

It was during the later months of 1813 that U.S. forces decided to withdraw from key locations along the Canadian side of the Niagara River. The former British stronghold of Fort George and its neighboring hamlets had been in American control, much to the disgust of the local population. Without an advanced warning to the inhabitants of the Village of Newark (present day Niagara on the Lake), orders were given for the community to be burned to the ground on December 15th, 1813. American commanders decided to enact a scorched earth policy in order to deprive sustenance and cover for the approaching British forces. However, this atrocity also meant that the civilians who lived in the village would have no shelter or provisions to help them survive the harsh Niagara winters. The horrific results of this action incensed British officials and a harsh military response was planned. On December 18th, 1813, a daring British attack across the frozen Niagara

River culminated in the fall of Fort Niagara. This would set the stage for a campaign that would lead to the burning of the Village of Buffalo on December 30th, 1813.

Buffalo Burns

The Saga of Job Hoisington

After landing and burning the village of Black Rock, the forces of Great Britain approached Buffalo along the old Guide Post Road (a portion of which is now Porter Avenue) and headed to Main Street where it was met by U.S. forces. However, these raw recruits would prove no match for the well-disciplined British troops. After holding the line for only a short time, they broke ranks, leaving the village and its inhabitants virtually defenseless with the exception of a few small militia units.

It is said that among those stalwart men stood the fifty-one year old carpenter and mason, Job Hoisington. He had come to Buffalo around 1811 and through hard and honest labor had built a fine reputation for himself. Unfortunately, his skills as a woodworker seemed to take on a more ominous task in early 1813 as he was commissioned to make pine coffins for some of the 300 soldiers who had died at the U.S. Encampment at Flint Hill.

The militia units stood their ground against the advancing redcoats for as long as they possibly could. Finally breaking under the mounting pressure, they began a retreat through the streets of the village. It was at the present day location of Porter and Plymouth Avenues that Job paused and said to his comrades, "I will have one more shot at them," and headed back towards the enemy. That was the last time that old Job Hoisington was seen alive.

It wasn't until the Spring of 1814 that Hoisington's body was found. The snows had begun to melt exposing scenes of horror as the remains of Buffalo's defenders began to be found in the mud and water of the thaw. As was the custom of warring Indians, his remains had been mutilated, scalped, and his outer clothing stripped from his body. As his face was blackened and crushed, Job's wife, Sarah, could only identify him from his name that was written on his undergarments. His skull had been perforated by a single musket ball and there were marks that had been left behind from three blows of a tomahawk. The body of Job Hoisington was buried in the nearby Cold Springs Cemetery.

There he lay for thirty-five years until the property was needed for the expansion of Buffalo in the mid 1800s. The bones from this small cemetery were exhumed, boxed, and reburied at Forrest Lawn. But for Job, his saga doesn't end there. It seems that because of his heroic status as well as the damage that his assailant had inflicted, his skull

Site of Job Hoisington's Death.

may have been taken as a curiosity. Another explanation was that someone in the medical profession overseeing the exhumations realized its value and took it home to be added to a macabre collection of body parts. It was not uncommon during this time period for skulls that bore the wounds of combat to be collected and studied by generations of medical students.

Over the many years since his heroic death, Job Hoisington has been spotted wandering the modern streets near the former cemetery. Could it be that he is looking to take that "one last shot" as he had wished? Or perhaps it may be that his headless body is still searching for the skull that was spirited away during reburial.

Today, a public marker, dedicated in May of 2008, has been placed in front of the Karpeles Manuscript Museum at Porter and Plymouth Avenues where that gallant Hoisington fell. It stands as a memorial to the selfless actions of a citizen soldier who answered the final call.

The Two Graves of Sarah Lovejoy

The wife of militiaman Joshua Lovejoy was said to be a force to be reckoned with. While the other occupants of Buffalo fled their homes during the attack, the thirty-five year old stubbornly stood alone against the onslaught of the British Indian Allies. It was common knowledge among frontier people that payment for Indian participation in military campaigns were scalps and any items that could be carried away and taken back to their remote woodland communities. Since her arrival in Buffalo, she and her family had struggled to create a home and now Sarah would be damned if anyone was going to plunder it.

As the chaos of war swept down Main Street, her neighbor Mrs. St. John cried out, "Don't risk your life for property!" To this, Sarah's obstinate reply was, "When my property goes, my life shall go with it!"

Unfortunately for Mrs. Lovejoy, her words rang true that day. She was last seen struggling with a warrior who was said to be removing curtains from a window. Sarah attacked the offending marauder with a carving knife reportedly cutting his arm. It was at that moment that survivors say the warrior raised his tomahawk and quickly ended Sarah's life.

According to folklorist Mason Winfield, as the madness began to wane, the few remaining neighbors entered the now-looted home. They were able to remove the corpse of Mrs. Lovejoy just as a squad of men arrived with the intent of setting fire to the home. Once thought ablaze, the men continued on, but the flames were extinguished by these same neighbors. Sarah's remains were then taken back into her house and laid upon a bedstead.

In death, Sarah was remembered to have been wearing a black satin dress and had long ebony hair that fell to the floor through the bed's now barren rope cords. Unfortunately, later when the nearby St. John Hotel was set on fire, the Lovejoy house burned with it.

As the smoke from the ruins slowly cleared, Joshua returned and lovingly collected the cremated remains of his late wife. He placed the cracked and blackened bones gently in a handkerchief for burial.

A marker has been placed in the Lovejoy plot at Forest Lawn that reads, "Sarah Johnson Killed By Indians at the burning of Buffalo, December 30th 1813." (Johnson was Sarah's maiden name.) It is here that the tragic story of Sarah Lovejoy could end, except it seems that her remains do not repose in Buffalo at all. There is a second grave marker in the Caledonia Mumford Cemetery some fifty miles east of the attack and bears this inscription, "Sarah Johnson, wife of Joshua Lovejoy, Born October 21,1771, Was killed by the Indians at the Burning of Buffalo, December 30, 1813." It seems that her husband had never buried his wife with the rest of his family. Joshua had taken Sarah's bones to be interred in the same plot as her sister.

Opposite page: Site of Sarah Lovejoy's House.

Many researchers have wondered if it is not Sarah who is in Forest Lawn, is there someone else who lies beneath the headstone? The answer is probably not. It was a common practice among many families to place a memorial marker in a family plot for a relative whose body may be lost or is buried at another location. The monument standing at Forest Lawn is called a "Cenotaph." Simply defined it means a monument to someone who is interred elsewhere but needs to be remembered or memorialized.

With her stubbornness, violent death, and cremation, you would think that Sarah Lovejoy would have had more than enough of wandering this earthly plane. There is yet one small incident that needs to be told. It seems that the modern-day Ellicott Square Building is located upon the spot where the Lovejoy home once stood. There has been a story that has circulated among paranormal investigators about a woman with long dark hair who has been seen wandering the halls of that building. Could this be the restless spirit of Sarah Lovejoy?

A Refuge in the Wilderness

The Hull House

Many of the demoralized survivors of the December attack on Buffalo were forced to make their way along the Genesee Road. Their goal was to seek the safety and shelter of the outlying farming communities. One of the beacons of hope along this path was the home of Warren and Polly Hull located in Lancaster, New York. The Hull home is a two-story, stone, Federal-style structure which was popular during the early 1800s. It was here that many shaken survivors would rest until it was safe to return to the ashes of their former community.

The historic Hull House, now a restored museum, is the oldest existing stone dwelling in Erie County. Also of interest is the nearby family cemetery which was heavily vandalized during the 1980s and is located on the property. Because of the extensive damage, only one stone stands in its original location from the possible twenty burials located there. During the restoration process, Ground Penetrating Radar was employed which resulted in the location of eighteen of the graves. Of those who have been rediscovered, it is impossible to know whose name is attached to which grave.

There have been several stories that have circulated about the old Hull House. Mysterious knockings have been heard as well as phantom lights being seen. Most interesting is the report of a rocking chair that seemingly rocks by itself.

The Hull House.

Who causes these paranormal activities to occur is unknown. It may be the spirits of the Hulls themselves who have stayed behind to check on the restoration of their beloved home. Or could it be the restless souls who lie buried in the family cemetery whose markers have been desecrated? What is known for sure is that this lovely building has now been preserved for generations to come and will continue to be a haven for those who once lived or visited its warming embrace.

The Lost Soldiers of the Garrison Cemetery

The sleepy community of Williamsville, New York became an important safe haven for those who survived the burning of Buffalo. As the defense of the Niagara Frontier was in peril, both civilian and military alike withdrew to the safety of inland military posts. Hospitals that were also near the front lines began to evacuate the sick and wounded sending them to the hospital and log barracks that lined the old Garrison Road near Ellicott Creek.

Williamsville, then called "William's Mill" was founded by Jonas Williams and David Evans. Williams went onto establish a water mill and was eventually elected supervisor in 1808. In 1813, U.S. General Winfield Hancock's 6,000 troops were quartered along Main Street which made it at the time the largest populated area between Buffalo and Batavia.

While any military hospital of the 1800s was primitive at best, Dr. Joseph Lovell, an outstanding medical officer, was placed in charge and did what he could to improve conditions. While he and those who labored under him attempted to save the lives of both U.S. soldiers as well as British prisoners of war, common diseases of the day began to slowly take their tolls upon the ranks crowded into the cold, wooden buildings. Poor sanitary conditions quickly led to the misery of the men causing diarrhea, pneumonia, dysentery, and typhus fever which proved to be the post's main killers.

As the illnesses began to mount, so did the losses. Not wishing for the diseased remains of soldiers to be placed so close to a populated area, it was requested that they find another spot in which to bury the dead. A nearby farmer donated some swampy land at the rear of his property for the military burial ground. It would be in this plot that over 200 men from both sides would be buried in open-slit trenches. Of course officer remains were normally attempted to be singularly buried as was the custom of war, however this was not always possible.

So there the dead remained undisturbed except for the occasional cart and the passing of time. It has been reported that the area where the Canadian Militia and Scottish Highlanders were buried was washed away when Ellicott Creek flooded and changed its course. We also know that the existing graves in the cemetery were "re-mounded" by a well-meaning War of 1812 Centennial Commission which caused much confusion as to the actual positioning of the burials. Another change to the landscape was the paving and construction of Aero Drive which may now cover a portion of the actual cemetery. This small parcel of land was given to the Township of Cheektowaga after the construction of the nearby New York State Thruway and is responsible today for its upkeep.

The ghosts of war are frightening no matter how they may have died Those who are buried at the old post hospital cemetery may still be seen walking, seeking loved ones or a reason to why they are still there. Having personally known families who lived nearby gave me some insight as to the reports of activity from that location. There has been an account of a "luminous" figure who has been seen standing on the creek side of the road. Could this be the spirit of a fallen British soldier? Also several nearby businesses have reported mysterious mists and objects that move on their own.

In 2009, I downloaded detailed topographical and satellite maps of the area around the cemetery in order to conduct an investigation of my own. With these maps I wished to ascertain if there may be any actual burials that were under Aero Drive itself or in the immediate area. Map dowsing is a process where the dowser uses both a pendulum

War of 1812 Military Cemetery.

Author dowsing with rods.

as well as pointer as he "works" on a map which has been divided into small sections. Holding the pendulum in one hand, the dowser touches each section of the map. In the case of looking for burials, when an area is touched where they may possibly be, the pendulum will register a "reaction" such as strongly spinning or moving from side to side. When I "dowsed" the cemetery location map, I found that indeed there was a strong "reaction," especially under the road, as well as where the creek "elbowed" nearest the cemetery. To me this meant that there were actual graves located there, but it is doubtful that they will ever be unearthed.

An Associated Press article that was dated May 8th, 2002, reported that Cheektowaga was attempting to have the cemetery included in the National Register of Historic Places. Using Ground Penetrating Radar it was concluded that there was indeed "disturbances in the ground" that was indicative of a burial ground. It achieved that status later in the year.

As cars drive by and planes from the nearby airport fly overhead, those who died at the nearby military hospital lie sleeping in the eternal night of death. May those spirits who still walk Aero Drive understand that their sacrifices were not in vain. Sentiments of the time have been summarized by the words of Secretary of the Treasury Albert Gallatin in 1816. "The war has renewed and reinstated the national feelings and character which the Revolution had given, and which were daily lessened. The people . . . . are more American; they feel and act more as a nation; and I hope the permanency of the Union is thereby better secured."

Location where British and Canadian Militia graves were washed away.

Chapter 5

A Place of Life
A Place of Death

Old Fort Niagara

The guns that once belched smoke and fire have now fallen silent. The surviving stone ramparts tell of a time when a vast wilderness empire had become the battleground for two warring European Nations. When contemplating the haunted legacy that is left to us by Old Fort Niagara, it is important to understand its significance to the history of America. Located in present-day Youngstown, New York, it has enjoyed a very bloody, yet exciting, existence.

The name Niagara is said to have originated from the name of a nearby Iroquois town known as "Ongniaahra" which meant the "point of land cut in two." Stone-Age Native Americans used the site as a hunting camp and most probably a place to rest when traveling on the ancient portage trail that snaked around Niagara Falls. So extensive was this trail that it reached from New England, past Niagara Falls, to Erie, Pennsylvania, and then north to the lands of the Mid-West and down to the Gulf of Mexico. A burial mound that was excavated in nearby Lewiston, New York, revealed a wealth of artifacts ranging from Neolithic flint "blanks" used for stone tool making to the teeth of a shark. The early European explorers immediately knew the importance of this natural route and sought measures to control and exploit it for their own purposes.

In 1678, the famous French Explorer Rene-Robert Cavelier La Salle constructed a small stockade called Fort Conti where the present-day fort now resides. This early enclosure would become a supply base while the construction of the early sailing vessel *Griffon* was taking place. This ship was the first European-built vessel to sail the Great Lakes. Unfortunately, this structure burned shortly after La Salle had left to explore the hinterlands and was abandoned.

The local inhabitants of the region were the Seneca Nation known as the "Keepers of the Western Door." They were part of a mighty coalition of tribes called the "Haudenosaunee" or the "Iroquois Confederacy." The Iroquois were extremely intelligent in both the ways of war and diplomacy. They knew that it was in their best interests to work with both the French as well as the English who now struggled to rule their slivers of land along the Great Lakes and the coasts of the Atlantic Ocean. Also important were the trade goods that were provided by the traders of these nations. Wool replaced furs and leather, iron strikers could easily create fire, steel knives were far superior to ones made of stone, and muskets could easily kill game replacing bows and spears.

In 1687, the Governor of New France (French Canada), the Marquis de Denonville, attempted to stem competing British colonial interests by using the Indian lands between their colonies as a buffer. To do this he established a military presence and built a new enclosure at the site of La Salle's former base aptly called Fort Denonville. Life on the Niagara frontier was brutal at best, and during the inhospitable winter months, all but twelve men of the men garrisoned there died from starvation and disease. By spring, the fort was then considered untenable and was abandoned. It is believed that the graves of these first soldiers were found when the fort began renovations in 1929.

The "Castle" of Old Fort Niagara. *Photo by Geoff Harding.*

To appease the Seneca, it became necessary to establish a place where trade could be conducted. At Niagara, a deal was brokered with tribal leaders to build a trade house, nicknamed "The House of Peace" on which construction began in 1726. However, this was no mere frontier trade post; instead, it was a marvel of military technology. Referred to as a "Machicolated House," its walls were made of thick stone, the widow shutters opened to the inside of the building so they could be easily closed if attacked and had possessed slots in them called "loops" so muskets could be fired through. The second floor overhung the first floor's outer walls and had openings where boiling oil or musket fire could rain down upon those attempting to breach its entry ways. Garrison rooms for soldiers were also constructed inside the building and it possessed its own powder magazine, kitchen, well, and chapel. This building essentially was a medieval citadel.

By the 1750s, tensions between the French and English were heightened as a European war spilled over onto North American soil. The French and Indian War, as it was called here in North American, was a nasty affair that would ravage frontier settlements. By 1759, the forces of Great Britain had besieged Fort Niagara. Its defenders held out for nineteen days, and knowing that the relief column sent from Detroit had been attacked and turned back, French Commandant Pierre Pouchot surrendered the fort.

Once in British control, the fortification experienced many new improvements. The defenses of the old French fort had been made up mostly of wooden palisades and mounded earth which became labor intensive to keep up. Forgoing this work, they decided to construct two massive stone "redoubts" thus creating "mini forts within a larger fort." A redoubt is often called a blockhouse and is created to be as self contained as possible. Two are usually constructed having a clear range of fire or a "dead zone" between them that protects a vulnerable section of a fort. Also these redoubts would serve as safe havens for those who worked or lived outside of their walls.

At the time of the Revolutionary War, the fort was used mostly as a supply depot and a center for Indian allies to gather and refit before going off on war parties, attacking settlements loyal to the new government. In 1779, General George Washington, in response to the massacres and burning of these border settlements, decided to mount a military expedition and destroy the heartland of the now-allied Iroquois. Starting just below modern-day Elmira, New York, this force would lay waste to all of the Indian towns, farms, orchards, and homes along its path to the Great Lakes. This would deprive the families of the Indian warriors much-needed shelter and food and would force these non combatants to English supply posts such as Fort Niagara. Called the Sullivan-Clinton Campaign, this action would leave in its wake a blackened scar upon the land.

Fleeing Native Americans made their way north, quickly becoming a problem for their English friends. With the winter season approaching and knowing and that the frozen waterways would end shipping, the refugees were offered to be taken to another location. However, many leaders refused, insisting that this was their land and they would not leave it. The winter of 1779 was one of the worst on record. Freezing temperatures caused much misery and supplies began to rapidly dwindle. Those Iroquois who arrived late in the season were forced to live in bark huts which provided meager protection from the harsh Lake Ontario winds. It is said that the resulting refugee camp was almost five miles in length and that it is possible that 3,000 or more men, women, and children may have perished.

In the spring, burial details were sent out, but in most cases, all that could be done was to spread quick lime over the corpses and pile brush on top of them. So terrible was the result of the campaign that Seneca mothers quiet their crying children by saying, "Shhhhh, Town Burner Will Hear You." Town Burner is the name given to General Washington by the Iroquois because of the results of that campaign.

It was not until the War of 1812 that Fort Niagara once again would face the smoke of battle. The new campaigns fought on the Niagara Frontier were full of atrocities on both sides. In 1813, U.S. forces were ordered to withdraw from the Canadian side of the Niagara River,

The Jesuit Chapel, located on the second floor of the Castle.

abandoning Fort George and the nearby village of Newark (Niagara On The Lake). While American orders included that time be given for the inhabitants to leave, this was ignored and U.S. troops set fire to the village in early December. The devastation on the local populace was immense leading to a cry of revenge to be uttered by British officials.

After the Americans military had abandoned their positions on Canadian soil, Crown troops incensed by the depredations at Newark crossed the river on the evening of December 19th, 1813. Keeping the element of surprise, the British were ordered not to fire a shot and used the cold steel of bayonets to dispatch the sleepy American pickets along the road. Eventually reaching Fort Niagara and forcing their way through the gates, the British fought its defenders literally from building to building. With the memory of Newark fresh in their minds, no quarter was given. In the "Red Barracks," they met with stiff resistance from armed hospital patients who were recovering there. Finally overtaken, these sick and wounded men were quickly dispatched by the redcoats. Next, the Brits turned their attention to the heavily defended South Redoubt. Breaking through the thick wooden door, its soldiers were forced to retreat up the stairs to the second floor hotly contested by the British Infantrymen who soon overtook them. With no hope in sight and losing a redoubt, all that was left to do was surrender the fort. With Fort Niagara back in British hands, the next goal would be a retaliatory attack on the village of Buffalo, which happened on December 30th 1813.

The signing of the Treaty of Ghent signaled the end of the War of 1812, and possession of the battered fort fell once again into American hands. By 1825, Fort Niagara began to lose its prominence as the Erie Canal was opened and the ancient portage route was no longer the easiest way to transport goods around the falls. In 1826, the garrison was removed and only a caretaker was left to man its walls.

When the American Civil War erupted, the United States needed to once again protect its boarders from its old nemesis Great Britain. England had supported the South's bid for independence and supplied the Confederate forces with war materials. As the Dominion of Canada in the 1860s was still a part of the British Empire, there needed to be a watchful military presence in the Great Lakes region. Tensions between the two nations began to rise and Fort Niagara was again garrisoned seeing the construction of new walls and artillery casements.

By the 1870s, the original Fort Niagara literally became obsolete and its buildings were used as officer housing and warehouses. New construction took place outside of the old fort's enclosures which then served as a training facility. In the 1940s, it became a "reception area" for new recruits as well as a POW camp for German prisoners. By 1945, the facility was declared "surplus," becoming a home for veterans and briefly used as an anti-aircraft battery during the Cold War. The fort was officially deactivated in 1963.

Of Ghosts, Masons, and Mysteries

That Rascal Morgan!

The year 1826 saw a marked decrease in the role that Fort Niagara played on the Western New York region, however another drama was about to unfold. William Morgan who was a native of Batavia, New York, and a member of the Freemasons was forcibly kidnapped and promptly disappeared. Morgan had been planning to publish a book exposing certain secrets of Freemasonry for profit. At the time of the infamous "Morgan Affair," Freemasonry was a fraternal organization that was made up of all social classes. Within its ranks farmers, tradesmen, business entrepreneurs, and even presidents could be counted. So large was this organization that meeting places called Lodges could be found in major cities as well as in the smaller hamlets found dotted along the countryside.

William Morgan, a stone cutter, was described by many sources to have been a slacker who was always in constant debt and was a frequent visitor at the local taverns. Claiming that he was an accomplished Mason he offered to teach new recruits the rituals and principles of the organization, for payment of course. He was inducted into the York Rite Royal Arch degree at Leroy, New York, in 1825, but it is doubtful that he had actually completed the lower degrees needed to achieve this status. When a new Masonic chapter was being formed in Batavia his name was excluded from it rolls because of this controversy. This angered Morgan and he decided to write a book exposing the higher degrees of the order in retaliation of this slight. Lacking the financial backing for this endeavor he partnered with a small time newspaper owner named David Cade Miller and began his work.

Being frequently drunk, he often bragged about his book idea when visiting the local pubs, many who were owned by Masons, whereby this information reached the local Masonic leadership. On September 11th, 1826, Morgan, who was no stranger to a jail cell because of his non payment of debts, was arrested for "not returning" the shirt and cravat of a fellow Mason and was taken to Canandaigua to be incarcerated. He was freed by someone who paid his debt and was then forcibly taken away in a carriage while crying out, "Murder, murder." After making several stops, he was placed in the old powder magazine of Fort Niagara. A safe place as it's only caretaker was a Mason.

It is said that the local Masons wished to hand Morgan over to their Canadian counterparts so he could be placed on an ocean-going ship, captained by a Mason of course, and dumped overboard. Another variation is that he was to be given "hush money" and sent into Canada to start another life having his family join him there. The ending that most researchers now believe occurred was that after being taken to Fort Niagara and having the Canadian Masons refuse to have anything to do with the plot, the conspirators having no backup plans, rowed him out into Lake Ontario and tossed his roped and weighted body into its icy waters. Upon hearing of this incident, horrified members left Freemasonry in droves almost crippling the organization. While there is a great controversy over the identity of a body that washed ashore being Morgan's, there is no proof that he was actually murdered. The "Morgan Affair" and the occasional sighting of a ghost near the powder magazine seems to have earned its reputation as one of the mysterious incidents that are associated with Fort Niagara.

The Powder Magazine where William Morgan was held captive.

The Ghosts Of Old Fort Niagara

A location such as Fort Niagara with its long history of war and intrigue cannot help but possess a few fascinating ghost stories. Having been a volunteer there myself for a number of years, I have a few of my own to share. As a historic interpreter at the fort, I would dress up in the clothing from the mid 1700s and actually live the life of one of the post's inhabitants. Paranormal investigators will recognize this method as similar to the "Singapore Theory" where investigators dress, talk, or play the music of a suspected ghost's time period in order to illicit a response. I will admit that I witnessed a lot of activity when I did this.

To many, the old French Castle is considered to be the place where the most hauntings seem to occur. Its proximity to where the Niagara River meets Lake Ontario is considered a "power vortex" as its rushing waters act as a conductor for paranormal energies. I have found that many such places are ripe with possible ghostly activities. Once, when I was staying overnight, I heard heavy footsteps pacing back and forth on the second floor. In fact, once I mustered some courage and shouted, "Will you stop so I can sleep?" Apparently, whomever it was up there must not have liked my comment and the distinct sounds of heavy leather soled shoes began to echo as if walking down the stairs. I believe that was the only time that I decided that discretion was the better part of valor and left to sleep in my truck.

The fort would often host small events for the volunteer staff in the off season. During one such spring weekend, a small group had gotten together to enjoy a period crafts seminar. We worked on many period projects, but the most intense part of the weekend came when a road-kill deer that was donated to us was skinned, butchered, and cooked. After our evenings feast, I was taking two crockery jugs of cider down to the building's cellar. Suddenly, I felt a sharp burning sensation on the back of my right hand. It was so painful that it forced me to drop the jug, which broke on the floor. Immediately looking down, I saw a bright red mark about an inch and a half wide, by four inches long which raised quickly into a welt. While I have visited other haunted locations within the fort many times, I will admit that I have yet to go back down in the cellar.

Even on a calm day the waves that crash into the break wall near the Castle will usually lull the most alert investigator to sleep. It is this sound that may serve as a natural "white noise" generator that helps give substance to the voices of the discarnate. Once when I was attempting to sleep in the first floor garrison room, the waves did not sound like they normally did. They were somehow a bit more muffled than usual, and shortly thereafter, the sounds of a whispered conversation in the hall was heard. Suddenly, one of the voices turned into what I thought was someone gasping for air. Thinking that it may have been a fellow volunteer becoming ill, I jumped up and looked out in the darkness, and realized that no one there.

Another active area is the North Redoubt. On one occasion while I was sleeping on the second floor, I awoke to see a person dressed in a red shirt walking down the stairs. Since there were three of us in the building at the time, I figured that it probably was one of my comrades having to answer the call of nature. I heard the heavy wooden door open and shut, however, it was at this time that I heard the two distinct snores of my friends who were now both accounted for. Who was it that visited us and opened the barred door I cannot say.

As a longtime researcher, I can attest that there is not an exact time for paranormal phenomena to take place. Many tourists and volunteers have had experiences during the daylight hours. Historical Interpreter Geoff Harding told me that when he was younger, he witnessed a mysterious colonial soldier whose clothing and accouterments were quite correct for the time period, standing near Commandant Pouchot's room in the Castle. This "soldier" could have been a volunteer with the exception that he did not have a face.

Several years ago, a visiting priest, who happened to be a French and Indian War reenactor, decided that he would sleep in and later say a mass in the Jesuit Chapel that was located on the second floor of the Castle. I was told that he left very early in the morning after hearing the sounds of heavy benches being dragged about. The experience did not scare him off, however, he now sleeps in a tent during events and conducts an outdoor mass appropriately enough under the shadow of the Father Millet Cross, honoring the first Jesuit at the site on an overturned canoe.

Perhaps one of my earliest recollections of paranormal activity occurred during the mid morning when I was visiting the old French warehouse near the office. When I walked into the room, I felt an "unusual feeling" there. It almost felt "like the air on a humid or rainy day." After looking at a large-scale relief map, I noticed that the door had not shut all the way, and as I reached for the handle to close it, I felt as if my hand had passed through something that felt like "cotton candy." Pulling my hand back, I saw the door slam shut all on its own. (In Spiritualist belief's, this type of feeling usually accompanies "ectoplasm.")

I have also found that the outer, Civil War era, red brick casements and sally port seem to be quite active if the conditions are just right. Once as I was walking through the Sally Port to retrieve my historic interpretive gear, I was startled by a shadow person standing in the middle of the enclosure who seemed to turn and just float into the brick wall. My favorite experience in that location was when a friend and I visited the fort just as it opened. It was a very slow day for tourists and we virtually had the place to ourselves. Earlier we had conducted an EVP session on the third floor of the Castle and had captured the single word "stop." But it seems that day the major activity at Fort Niagara centered around the casemates. As we walked down the stairs, we both experienced the chill of a dull field of static electricity. Walking towards the casemate's powder magazine, the batteries in my digital camera went dead. I grabbed my back up camera which also quickly died. My friend started taking photo's and was able to get six shots off before his camera experienced the same fate as mine. We next attempted to conduct an EVP session but our recorder batteries also drained. Leaving the casemates and standing outside checking our gear, we found that the previously drained camera batteries now showed that they were back to half power. What is interesting about the experience is that in three of the six shots taken, there seems to be a white mist near the archway of the powder magazine. Could this have been a spirit that has lingered on and whose energy was disturbed when we entered? Again, I have no answer.

Members of the fort's staff have also reported many interesting stories. One remembers that on a very chilly spring day he was warming himself by the hearth in the Castle's old French kitchen. He heard the door of the Trade Room open and the sounds of shoes upon the stone floor. Looking up at a very large glass encased map that reflected the inside Trade Room, he noticed someone standing there. Thinking that it was a tourist, he went to greet them...and upon entering the room realized that there was no one there.

One of the more recent accounts to come out of Fort Niagara happened to a workman who was installing a display alarm in the Castle's Pouchot Room. Seeing something shining near his tool belt and thinking that his flashlight had somehow turned on, he looked down as saw a glowing orb that was floating waist high. Unnerved by the sight, he quickly ran across the parade ground seeking help and was accompanied back by a staff member. Again, as he worked the orb presented itself, but this time was witnessed by both of them as it floated out of the room and

Entrance to the Underground Civil War Casemates where
etheric mist has been experienced.

down the second floor hallway. Most researchers and volunteers agree
that the second floor near the former Commandant's room is by far the
most haunted due to the fact that the floors were never replaced but
only stabilized during the building's restoration because of the stone
powder magazine beneath it.

When it comes to Fort Niagara, one never knows where all of the bodies are buried. It seems that the installation of new water and gas lines have in the past exposed unmarked graves. Once during such a project, the remains of two Caucasian women and a child were unearthed. Unfortunately, there is no record of these burials that have been found.

The post cemetery is situated within an easy walk from the fort. Here lie the dead of many eras, how many is uncertain. During the Victorian age, boaters while enjoying a leisurely ride down the Niagara River would often see that the eroding river wall of the cemetery exposed, the burial grounds deteriorating coffins, and an assortment of bones. The sight was so appalling that the wall was fixed and the bones gathered and reburied. The cemetery has also been a past gathering point for people of eclectic beliefs. Once a volunteer who had arrived in the late evening reported seeing a group of people in what he described as white robes were doing a sort of "Snake Dance" within the burial grounds fence. Their purpose is still unknown and they have not been witnessed since. Also, occasionally, a woman in white is seen floating over the graves.

With the coming of Fall, thoughts of ghosts, and goblins, and things that go bump in the night seem to take center stage. For one young newspaper reporter, an October trip to Fort Niagara served as a frightening experience. His published article begins with the sentence, "Only an idiot could've come up with an idea like this." After getting a tour of the fort from Bob Emerson, the site's Executive Director, he was left alone to his own devices in the Castle. Soon the sounds of heavy footsteps and a door being slammed shut were heard. Knowing of the site's haunted reputation, he decided that it may not be prudent to go and check the rest of the building for

Fort Niagara Post Cemetery

a possible intruder. Calling Emerson, he stated that he enough material for an article and that he was ready to leave. When Bob arrived, they both checked the Castle to see if anything was amiss but found nothing. While this reporter did ask permission to attempt to stay overnight again, he stated that he would do so only with "2 or 35 of his closest friends."

Today, Old Fort Niagara is part of the New York State Office Of Parks, Recreation, and Historic Preservation and is lovingly administered to by

the Old Fort Niagara Association. It is because of its staff and dedicated corps of volunteers that we today are able to understand and relive our region's sometimes turbulent past. Fort Niagara's walls may be no longer needed to protect a wild frontier, but to its ghostly residents it is a place where their memories are cherished and the dead are welcomed to walk.

Chapter 6

Seneca Witchcraft and Christian Pioneers

"Go to Salem! Look at the records of your own government, and you will find that hundreds have been executed for the very crime which has called forth the sentence of condemnation of this woman, and drawn down upon her the arm of vengeance. What have our brothers done more than the rulers of your people have done?"
~Seneca Chief Red Jacket
Addressing the jury during the murder trial of Tommy Jemmy,
July 1821

Witchcraft is often defined as the use of sorcery for malevolent purposes. During ancient times, entire populations would shutter in fear just from the mention of the subject. However, during these "days of enlightenment," many of us do not take the actual existence of the "craft" very seriously. The term itself may only conjure up fanciful images of black-clad women wearing pointed hats, having gathered around a bubbling cauldron. However, at the turn of the nineteenth century, witchcraft was still a topic that many people would attempt to avoid.

To the Seneca tribesmen of the Iroquois Confederacy who had backed the British during the Revolutionary War, a dark and evil age had begun. A once-proud tribal society, they were now reduced to a defeated people forced to live in poverty upon government mandated reservations. Deprived of ancestral lands by a conquering army, a mentality of defeatism, as well as sickness and alcoholism spread rapidly throughout this once-prominent nation. To many, an evil curse had been levied upon the "Keepers of the Western Door."

Within the early culture of the Iroquois, no injury or death was thought of as accidental or resulting from natural origins. The balance of good and evil was a part of daily life. There was a belief that even a good person could in fact invoke evil entities which brought forth natural disasters and the loss of life. In their minds, such evil deeds could not pass unanswered bringing about an almost endless cycle of intertribal feuding and warfare. Just as in countless cases before, aboriginal witchcraft was readily found in the social structures of the post Revolutionary Seneca Nation.

In May of 1821, a Seneca woman by the name of Kau–qua–tau was found dead upon a path near Buffalo Creek, a victim of a violent attack. (The location is believed to be near the foot of modern-day Hamburg Street in Buffalo, New York.) A deep wound to her neck was determined to be the cause of her demise. Much attention to this incident was paid by tribal and white leaders alike. Kau–qua-tau was no ordinary murder victim. She had been earlier found guilty of witchcraft and sentenced to death.

From the scant records left to us from that time, we know that Kau–qua–tau lived in a small cabin near "Jack Berry's Town" on what is now modern Main Street in West Seneca, New York. Consulting William L. Stones work, "The Life and Times of Red Jacket," we find the following description of the incident:

> In the Spring of the year just mentioned (1821), a Seneca Indian fell into a state of languishment and died. The character of the disease were such that the medicine men did not understand it; and from a variety of strange circumstances attending the sick man's decline and death, it was sagely concluded that he had been destroyed by sorcery. Nay more, the woman who had nursed him and anxiously watched him at his bed-side was fixed upon as the beldam who, by the aid of an evil spirit, had compassed his death.

Fearing for her life Kau–qua–tau fled to Canada. As the Seneca were living on reservations within the confines of the new United States, they did not have the authority to order her back to face these charges. In her absence, a council was held where she was found guilty and was to be summarily executed. Once again we turn to William L. Stone's work to describe what happened.

> But the Indians were too well informed and wary to carry the execution into effect beyond the confines of their own territory, either in Canada or the United States. The poor culprit was therefore artfully invited back to the American side of the Niagara, and hence within the bounds of their own jurisdiction where it was determined that she would meet her doom. Still the Indian who had been designated as executioner faltered in his duty. Either his heart or his hand failed, or his conscience smote him, and he declined the fulfillment of his bloody commission. In this emergency a chief named So – on – on – gise, but who was usually called Tommy Jemmy, seized a knife, and dispatched the sorceress by cutting her throat.

Upon the discovery of the woman's corpse, an arrest warrant was issued for Tommy Jemmy, however, the local constable was afraid to carry out this duty. A man by the name of Pascal Pratt, reputedly on friendly terms with the Seneca and who also spoke their language, agreed to find the Seneca leader and serve it. He found Tommy Jemmy at Chief Red Jacket's house. After an explanation of the warrant, Red Jacket calmly asked Pratt when and where they should appear.

Tommy Jemmy was brought to trial in Buffalo, New York, in July of 1821. His main defense for his actions was that Kau–qua–tau had been accused of witchcraft and was formally condemned to death by the assembly of chiefs. He had merely carried out the sentence.

The renowned Seneca orator Red Jacket stepped up to Tommy Jemmy's defense. In fiery tones he spoke of witchcraft:

> What! Do you denounce us as fools and bigots, because we still believe that which yourselves believed two centuries ago? Your black-coats thundered this doctrine from the pulpit, your judges pronounced from the bench, and sanctioned it with the formalities of law; and you would now punish our unfortunate brother for adhering to the faith of his fathers and of yours! Go to Salem! Look at the records of your own government, and you will find that hundreds have been executed for the very crime which has called forth the sentence of condemnation of this woman, and drawn down upon her the arm of vengeance. What have our brothers done more than the rulers of your people have done? And what crime has this man committed by executing in a summary way, the laws of his country, and the command of the Great Spirit.

Upon deliberations, the jury ruled that the Seneca were in fact an independent nation and that the local authorities had no jurisdiction over the case. The Buffalo court, however, did refer the case to the Supreme Court of New York, which took up the question of Seneca sovereignty, but were unable to render a judgment. They referred the case to New York Governor DeWitt Clinton who proposed a legislative solution. A law was then passed on April 22, 1822, which asserted that New York had the "sole and exclusive jurisdiction" of punishing criminals for the crimes that they committed within the boundaries of the state. The legislature also acknowledged that Tommy Jemmy's act had been done "under the pretense of authority derived from the councils of the chiefs, sachems, and warriors" of the Seneca Nation and under these "circumstances" it seemed expedient to grant him a pardon. Thus the executioner was set free.

The History of the Old Ebenezer Community

In 1826, after much debate, the lands of the former Buffalo Creek Reservation were sold and opened to new settlement. The area was eventually bought by a German Christian sect called the "Community of True Inspiration" who purchased the former Indian lands, existing homes, and sawmills that dotted the area. The name chosen for the area was "Ebenezer" which originated from the First Book of Samuel – chapter 7, verse 12. It states:

> Then Samuel took a stone, and set it between Mispeh and Shen, and called the name of it Ebenezer, saying, Hitherto hath the Lord helped us.

Christian Metz, an early church leader and "Werkzeug" (prophet/channel), exclaimed the name while in a "state of spiritual animation":

> Ebenezer you shall call it
> Hitherto our Lord has helped us
> He was with us on our journey
> And from many perils saved us
> His path and way are wonderful
> And the end makes clear the start

Today, the location of the former community encompasses the hamlets of Upper Ebenezer (Blossom, New York), Middle Ebenezer (Gardenville, New York) and Lower Ebenezer (situated near the intersection of Seneca Street and Union Road). There were many legal obstacles that the community had to overcome, one being the eviction of Native Americans, many of which were in residence upon the lands. In May of 1844, Christian Metz under a state of anxiety had a disturbing dream:

> The night following the council, two Indians seemed to come, as he drowsed, and to attempt to bind him. On awakening he no longer saw the Indians but a Moor (a Negro) stood before him with a rope in his hands and asked: "Shall I hang you?" Metz sprang from his bed to defy him and the figure disappeared.

This dream, hallucination, or whatever, illustrates the general effect produced by the protracted difficulties at that time.

Eventually, the legalities of land purchase were finalized to the satisfaction of the lawyers representing the Seneca people and the colonists took possession of the lands. As the new arrivals trickled into the colony, the need for shelter became an important consideration. We know that there were over twenty buildings that were in existence ready to temporarily house the colonists and all were immediately pressed into service. However, one cabin would become a hellish nightmare to those who lived within its walls.

The Haunted Cabin and Cemetery

Those living near the old "witch cabin" had an aversion to the place. The story of the murder of Kau-qua-tau was still well known by both the white and native inhabitants living on the former Buffalo Creek Reservation. After the grisly discovery of the alleged witch's mutilated corpse, it was taken back to her cabin, and as legend would have it, buried beneath the earthen floor. This may be factual as the remains of a convicted witch would not be welcomed in any of the Indian or white burial grounds.

The first mention of the old cabin appears in Metz's journal detailing the funeral of a sect member who had passed. Metz wrote:

Old Main Street Cemetery, site of The Witch Cabin.

On June 19 (1845) Brother Jacob Sommer died in Lower Ebenezer at the age of 52. His was the first funeral held at the sacred place; as the congregation came to it every one kneeled to pray God that this might be blessed as a peaceful place, where previously many horrors had been seen. An old Indian cabin had stood here and many outrageous deeds had been committed.

The mythology of this haunted location has it that a family was assigned to live in the cabin as their own home was being built. While living in the structure, all manner of visions and apparitions appeared to them. Most unnerving was that of an Indian woman imprisoned in chains. Also, legend has it that the ground would shake and unearthly waling sounds could be heard. The family assigned there took matters into their own hands and began to question local Seneca's still living in the area. They were told of the murder and the subsequent burial under the floor of the cabin. Such was this family's horror that it prompted Christian Metz to personally make a visit to the site. He has left us an encrypted testimony that is found in a journal entry about his night spent in the cabin. Metz also is reported to have seen the ghostly "woman in chains." This experience prompted a call to the community's Elders who gathered to pray at the site and consecrate the ground so all who were buried there could "rest in peace." Part of that rite was recorded by Metz:

Metz Journal Entry – June 22, 1845

...that He may bring to an end all strife and quarrel, so that afterwards the precious fruit of the sweet peace of God may sprout and grow on the quiet soil of your hearts; I say bend your knees at the place of the grave at this time, and pray to the Lord your God in Silence. Although the departed soul is not worthy of this consideration there is something else, a deeper hidden meaning –

David's hero will drink of the brook in the way, therefore shall lift up his head, and the earth upon which thou has committed so many sins, shall, through your tears of repentance be atoned as between you and your God through the mediator. It has been a mute witness of so many horrors had been seen.

After the re-consecration of the site as a place of burial and peace, no other paranormal activities were experienced. Two years later, the cabin mysteriously burned to the ground. The "Ebenezers" erected a white picket fence around the site of the cabin and no community burials took place on that spot. Eventually, the colony decided to sell their lands and headed for their community located in Amana, Iowa.

Today, the Old Main Street Cemetery lies hidden behind overgrown bushes and wild roses. The fallen stones bear a silent testimony to the staunch German settlers who came in search of religious freedom and a place to create their own "Eden." To the rear of the cemetery merely a few feet from the top of the ridge that overlooks an athletic field, lay the remains of the first colonists as well as those of three Indians. Enclosed by a wooden fence, the area is quite overgrown with brambles and wild grape vines, and during the summer is a haven for ticks.

So where was the original cabin actually located? We may never know. However, there is an area directly in front of the Indian graves that seems to be devoid of headstones. Could this be the final resting place of Kau-qua-tau? Unless there is an archeological dig planned in the future, we will probably never know for sure. One thing is certain, reports that the Seneca witch's ghost still haunts us can be found to this very day. The prayers of Christian Metz and the community Elders may have only let Kau-qua-tau's spirit rest for a time. Perhaps it is not her at all. It just might be the memories of a once-noble people crying out for an age now past.

Early Ebeneezer graves are located behind the wooden fence.

A Case of Murder, Sex, and Witchcraft

The French sculptor Henri Marchand came to Buffalo in 1925 with his wife, Clothildie, and their five children. Marchand was hired by the Buffalo Museum of Science to produce the life-like dioramas that would serve as a hallmark of that institution. One of the projects that he was commissioned to do was to produce a diorama about the lives of the local Native population. He and Clothilde would often be found in a cabin on the Cattaraugus Reservation where he would study the lifeways of the local Seneca people and she collected plants for his work. Sometimes during the course of his research, he met a young Seneca/Cayuga woman named Lila Jimerson and she agreed to model for him. However Marchand was a lecher and professed a "necessity" to "make love" to his models as it was the only way that he could see these women naked. This he said was needed to make sure that his work was anatomically correct. Whether or not Clothilde knew of his unique method for accuracy is not known.

A popular saying is that "Hell hath no fury like a woman scorned." The proof of this was played out when Marchand's son stumbled upon a horrific scene when he returned home from school on March 6th, 1930. Clothilde lie motionless on the stairwell landing. Police were called in, and at first, it looked as if she had slipped and fallen down the stairs.

Later, after the Coroner examined her body, gashes were found on her head and she smelled of chloroform. Ruling the death a homicide, the Buffalo police immediately questioned Marchand and cleared him. They next began a routine investigation of anyone who had been associated with the family, including those on the reservation. It was there that they found out that the artist and his model were conducting an tawdry affair. When pressured, Lila implicated her friend, Nancy Bowen, an elderly woman in whose house was found the ear pieces to Clothilde's glasses as well as bloody clothing.

A trial was quickly convened. Overcome by this whirlwind of justice, Lila collapsed and was sent to the hospital. While there, she made a "sick bed" plea of guilty, but retracted it the next day. Her physicians said that she was too ill to continue and would not be able to leave the hospital for at least two weeks. Upon hearing this, the judge declared a mistrial.

Lila Jimerson's second trial definitely created a sensation among the elite of the City. Henri Marchand admitted the he had many such sexual affairs with his models and that Jimerson was but one of many. In fact, by the time the second trial got underway, he had already remarried, this time to an eighteen-year-old girl and was living comfortably in a country house near Albany, New York. This fact would not be lost on those who sat in judgment of the Indian women. Lila had also told the court that Henri had inquired about having reservation thugs kill his wife. While not damning to the women, it did shed some light on the character of the artist.

Another fact that came to light was that Jimerson had convinced old Mrs. Bowan that Clothilde was in fact a "white witch" and had something to do with the recent passing of her husband. This notion would be reinforced by the fact that Clothilde was often seen on the reservation picking wild mushrooms and "strange hellish vegetables." In the mind of the traditional culture of the Seneca, this could serve as proof that she was practicing witchcraft.

Another cultural point that needs to be made is that once a witch is discovered, she needs to be executed by either "clubbing or burning." When the police searched the Bowen home, they found items that were similar to the hammer that was believed to have been used to inflict the gashes on Mrs. Marchand's head. Testifying as sort of an expert witness, famed anthropologist Arthur C. Parker examined the items believed suspect and stated that they were the same type of items "used to expel evil spirits in accordance to Iroquois belief." The evidence was damning, however the tide of popular opinion sided with the scorned woman and her friend. The trials and deliberations lasted just under a year and Lila was found innocent. Nancy Bowen on the other hand was pronounced guilty of murder but was given the light sentence of time already served and released.

The case is still remembered by some who live on the Cattaraugus Reservation. Lila passed from this life in 1972. Her friend, Nancy, returned to her home, took care of her horses, farmed, and lived quietly until her death. While it is highly doubtful that Clothilde was a witch, it was she who paid for the sins of her husband. Henri Marchand died in 1953 at the age of 73. You may still see many of his dioramas today as they are on display at the Buffalo Science Museum.

Chapter 7

Buffalo's Infected District

Booze, Brawlers, and Soiled Doves

Following the War of 1812, the United States quickly realized the need for a protected inland waterway. It was thought that a canal which linked the Hudson River in Albany to the Great Lakes would efficiently transport both goods and immigrants seeking to settle on western lands. Begun in 1817 and completed in 1825, the Erie Canal not only brought prosperity to the nation, but also the many towns and cities along its path. Unfortunately for Buffalo, with that affluence came unscrupulous individuals and the canal's western terminus quickly became a haven for vice.

Reputably one of the worst locations along the waterway's route was Canal Street which bordered the actual canal and is today Marine Drive near the Buffalo Skyway. This area now hosts many apartment buildings, commercial properties, parking lots, and several waterfront attractions. In its heyday, Canal Street was a place of rest for the weary sailors who manned the mules and barges that brought the great prosperity to the region. Most of these men hardened by years of back breaking labor were ill tempered, drunken louts who craved whiskey, whores, and spoiled for a fight. To cater to this type of clientele, fifty-three buildings were constructed on Canal Street, thirty-nine of which were saloons, most having their own brothels. The waterfront was the subject of many 1800's newspaper articles stemming from the frequent riots, murders, and debauchery that took place there. It is little wonder why that area took on such names as "The Five Points," The Hooks," and "The Infected District."

Plying their trade along Canal Street could be found well-known personalities such as Pug Nosed Cora, and the woman who danced upon a twelve-inch-wide column Kitty O'Neill. Saloons such as "Fisty Carroll's" and "Mother Carey's Boarding House" provided entertainment of a more personal and sometimes dangerous nature. In fact, a story is told about a saloon that was once located next to Mother Carey's where the captain of a barge went in for a drink with his first mate. During the course of the visit, the Captain was lured into a back room where a trap door was opened exposing a gangway that led to a lower-level barroom. Suddenly, the door was closed behind him and bolted from the other side. Immediately he thought that he would end up like so many unfortunates who were fed drinks that were drugged, and after passing out, were tossed into the canal with heavy stones tied to their necks. The captain knew of these plots and quickly began buying the rogues drinks while pouring his cups down the side of his neck. He pretended to become drunk, and once all were inebriated, he was able to pull out his long-folding "Spanish Knife" hidden inside of his sleeve. He then forced the bartender to have the door opened so that he could make his escape.

It was these taverns and saloons that may have been the first destinations sought out by thirsty "canawlers." One such place called "Doug's Dive" was operated by a former slave by the name of William Douglas and located on Commercial Street just below the grade of the barge mules towpath. It was described as being infested with vermin and had the reputation of

Site of Canal Street.

having the most hardened of canal sailors as customers. The "dive's" interior was depicted as being putrid smelling and having shelves behind the bar that stocked an array of cracked glasses, dark bottles, and empty cigar boxes. Fittingly a couple of chairs, benches, and a long table added to its ambience while several semi-closed doors hid "canal toughs" waiting for the unknowing rube to wander their way. It is believed that the unflattering term "dive," which refers to any unsavory location, may have originated from such a canal saloon.

Law-breaking was rampant, and during the 1830 to 1836 time period, it was estimated that seventy to eighty percent of all crimes committed in the United States occurred along the Erie Canal. The highest proportions were found to have been in the Rochester and Buffalo canal districts. In fact, there were several areas of "The Infected District" that local law enforcement refused to enter. Adding to these statistics each year were the many bodies that were found in the canal after it was dredged to remove the silt that had accumulated over the winter months. It has also been reported that unwanted babies were often tossed into the canal to drown by their mothers who may have been addicted to alcohol and drugs, worked as prostitutes, or who just did not wish to care for a "bastard" child. It was a hard life, and death was a common place.

Terminus of The Erie Canal In Buffalo, New York.

While researching the Erie Canal Terminus I had he opportunity to interview a parking attendant who worked near the Marine Drive Apartments and along the former site of Canal Street. He related that one evening he was startled by the sounds of a woman crying nearby. Thinking that it may have been an injured tenant, he searched the area but found no one. Upon turning his gaze towards the direction of Marine Drive, he saw what can be described as a "woman in white." This specter was dressed in old-fashion clothing, seemed startled to apparently having been seen. The apparition then quickly disappeared.

Eventually, Canal Street saw many important changes. First, its name was changed to Dante Place when Italian immigrants began to settle in its squalid, disease-ridden tenements. In 1936, a gas explosion and subsequent fire destroyed the rat-infested neighborhood allowing for future development ventures once that section of the Erie Canal became obsolete and was filled in.

Buffalo, during the glory days of the Erie Canal, prospered because the influx of goods and immigrants coming to its region. Nevertheless, that growth was tempered by the suffering and civic pandemonium that was also created with it. Today, Buffalo's waterfront is beginning to experience a much-needed renaissance. Cobblestone streets that once felt the gate of horse hooves have been rediscovered and tourists now visit the spot where the once-mighty Erie Canal emptied its waters into the Great Lakes. For the people who lived and worked on old Canal Street, their spirits may still roam in the forlorn hope of finding a drink of whiskey or the familiar sites of those chaotic days.

Chapter 8

Of Grease Paint And Broken Dreams

Lancaster Opera House

The months of April, May, and July of 1894, were devastating to the Town of Lancaster, New York. Along Central Avenue lie the charred skeletons of the once-thriving community. As the story goes, the only building left standing was the red brick town hall whose construction had been started earlier that year. Designed by George J. Metzger and built at the cost of $30,000, this fireproof structure served the community as both a town hall and as an opera house which opened in 1897. To the modern mind, this may pose a conundrum, however it was a common practice during this time period to build structures that would serve more than one purpose.

The stage of the opera house is similar to the ones used for Shakespearean productions having a "rake" or additional height added to every linear foot so the audience could see the actors both upstage as well as downstage clearly. In the 1920s and 1930s, musicals and traveling minstrel shows were often performed there. At the time of the Great Depression, the Opera House became a center for needy people to gather and receive food and clothing. In World War II, the ladies of the area used the dressing room as a place to sew parachutes which were packed on the hall's floor. Finally, during the era of the Cold War, it served as the regional Civil Defense headquarters. After the facility was transferred to the newly built underground shelter at Chestnut Ridge Park, the great hall and balcony was remodeled into offices and storage space.

In 1975, restoration of the opera house back to its original design were begun. Ceilings were repaired, the hall's wooden floor was refinished, and period-looking lighting fixtures installed. With the addition of a new staircase as well as an elevator, the restored Lancaster Opera House reopened its doors on September 20, 1981.

The Lancaster Opera House.

Throughout the years, tales of ghostly visitors have intertwined themselves with history and fact. One such story concerns a building caretaker who apparently suffered a heart attack while working in the bell and clock tower. It is he who enjoys making the elevator operate when there is no one else around. Another legend that persists is the one about the star-crossed lovers who may have performed at the Opera House. Their names were William and Priscilla, and as the story goes, they had a quarrel and broke up. William continued touring with the company and the heartbroken Pricilla left for home in Virginia. After a short time, William realized that he could not live without her and hurried to the Old Dominion State. Unfortunately, when he arrived, he found that she had been murdered.

It seems that their spirits may have come back to the Opera House where they may have experienced happier times. The local staff blames William each time they find papers shuffled, locked doors found open, and objects moved about. Pricilla is said to appear in the guise of a woman dressed in lavender and is seen often sitting on the right side of the balcony during performances.

Perhaps the most memorable paranormal occurrence happened in July of 1988, when during a performance a heavy TV set was seemingly "launched" into the air, arching over the footlights, and falling just shy of the first row. Amazingly, enough the TV even worked afterwards, attesting to the gentle way that it came to rest.

A building such as the Lancaster Opera House is a place of history, politics, and merriment. Plays that contain mystery, horror, and romance have a fitting place on its historic stage. Somehow, it is very appropriate that there are also ghosts who can call it home.

The Starry Night Theater

With productions such as *Night of the Living Dead*, *Danse Macabre*, and *Nosferatu* this former church seems to have carved out a well-deserved niche among horror aficionados. However, are all of the patrons who walk through its doors still among the living? Designed by George Fischer of the architectural firm of Gombert and Thompson, its cornerstone was appropriately laid on October 31st, 1890. This beautiful building boasts an 80-foot steeple and had seating for almost 400 congregates. Its owners, the "Deutsche Vereinigte Evangelische Friedens Gemeinde," which translated means "German United Evangelical Peace Congregation," served German immigrants of the Methodist faith. After the building of the Erie Canal, the congregation split off from their parent religious organization and formed the "Frieden's United Church of Christ" or "Free Church." In 2001, it was sold by the congregation to the Starry Night Theater, Inc. and renamed the Ghost Light Theater.

The Starry Night Theater.

The theater's interior is a Gothic masterpiece and its owners took great strides not to hide the original church. With high ceilings, dark wood columns, and organ loft, it gives theater patrons a sense of playful foreboding. Along with its dark atmosphere, there seems to be no shortage of otherworldly activity. Loud unexplained noises are heard, the sounds of breathing, chairs moving, and voices in the distance seem to be common place. Also an eerie feeling of being watched is whispered among both the cast and crew. This location has been investigated by several paranormal investigative groups and frequent cold spots, partial apparitions, and K-2 spikes are reported.

When attending a play in 2009, I had my own personal experience. While in the lower level where a lounge and snack bar are located, I turned a corner and saw what I believe to have been a shadow person. As the curtain was about to rise, I was down in that area almost entirely alone. I remember walking towards the back of the lounge and saw a "mass" that blacked out the wall behind it and seemingly disappeared before my eyes.

Could the phenomena that takes place at the Starry Night Theater be former church members stopping by to take a look at what their old place of worship has become? Or perhaps it is just the residual emotions of countless patrons who have enjoyed the hard work and dedication of those who strive to present quality productions for an appreciative audience? In either case this theater is a paranormal diamond.

The Riviera Theater

Of the many entertainment halls that once graced the Niagara region, the Riviera Theater remains a battered survivor of an age when grace and beauty once influenced the cinematic world. Built in 1926 on Webster Street in North Tonawanda, this 1,100 seat theater was designed by the architectural firm of Leon H. Lambert & Sons and nicknamed the "Showcase of the Tonawandas." In an age of silent movies, a locally manufactured Wurlitzer Pipe Organ was installed for musical accompaniment as well as public recitals. So grandiose was the nature of this theater that the organ's main console was painted to match the Italian Renaissance motif of the building's interior. It must be acknowledged that the significance of this musical instrument was monumental in an age where the actors were voiceless and soundtracks non existent. The "Mighty Wurlitzer Organ" was specially built to give a vast array of magical sounds which added life to the images projected on the silver screen.

During the Great Depression, "the Riv" was sold to the Shea's Theater Company who officially changed its name to "Shea's Riviera." Over the years, it has served many incarnations, such as a dance hall for teens, a movie theater, and a concert hall. After being sold several more times, it was finally purchased by the Niagara Frontier Organ Society who has been working to restore both the organ as well as the theater to its original magnificence. On April 22, 1980, The U.S. Department of the Interior placed The Riviera Theater on the Register of Historic Landmarks.

When it comes to show business, we find that those who not only act but also work within the entertainment industry itself can be a superstitious lot. All one needs to do is to simply ask anyone associated with the Riviera Theater and they will tell you that it abounds with stories of strange noises, phantom stagehands, and even a small girl named Mary whose footsteps have been heard repeatedly running up and down the aisles.

Para-X Radio Host John Crocitto was invited to be a part of an investigation that took place at "The Riv" and came away with some very interesting experiences. It seems that after setting up the infra red cameras and "going dark," he immediately heard whispered voices coming from the balcony. Checking it out, he found no one up there. John next decided to try an audio "ghost box" session. A "ghost box" is simply a digital radio that has been modified to scan AM or FM frequencies. Turning the radio receiver on and letting it scan for a few minutes he asked if there was

The Riviera Theater.

anyone who would like to talk to him. A few seconds later as if heard in a "real time" conversation the following answer came, "We Are Coming." This discarnate voice seemed to be that of a middle-aged woman. When John asked how many spirit people were there with her, the same voice related that there were "five spirits" in the theater. Later in the session, when discussing the balcony with another paranormal investigator, the word "Up" was issued from the radio. The voice this time seemed to be from a very old woman. This was immediately followed by a loud bang that sounded as if it came from the projection room. Upon entering the projection, booth it was clear that there had been no one in the booth at the time of the sound.

Next John proceeded to investigate the dressing rooms, as there have been many creepy sounds reported as well as the sightings of strange shadows that seem to move. As he entered the first room, the hair on his arm stood up as if he had passed through an electrical current. This is a common occurrence found at many haunted locations. Naturally created energy becomes somehow trapped at locations and feeds into the manifestation of physical phenomena such as sounds and ghostly sightings.

The highlight of the investigation came when John became startled by a what he thought was the outline of a fellow investigator. Using a flashlight with a blue lens (which creates more contrast in ambient light), he saw the full outline of what he took to be a real person. John looked at him dead on as the apparition was in front of him. This was long enough to see that it appeared to be a male having very short hair. Surprisingly, the "shadow person" seemed to know that he had been spotted. It paused briefly, stood up straight, its image visually "shuttered" and then exited into thin air. What was extraordinary about this haunted encounter was that John was not the only one to witness it; three other investigators also saw it.

When reflecting upon John's experiences, I am reminded of a quote by Edgar Allen Poe, "All that we see or seem is but a dream within a dream." Theaters such as the historic Riviera are rich in both history as well as paranormal experiences. It seems that the ghostly gentleman that was seen by so many, may actually walk within his own world of dreams. There are several theories in the metaphysical world that spirits may become trapped within the time era of which they lived. Could it not be possible that sometimes, if the conditions are right, that "time" may somehow overlap causing the past and present to seem as if one? Perhaps this is why the "shadow man" seemed startled and disappeared when "he" perceived John. To him John may have been the specter? Whatever the reason, this wonderfully restored theater seems to be the home to those who love her now as much as its original patrons who passed many a Friday evening watching the celluloid marvels of a new age.

Shea's Buffalo Theater

Michael Shea was born in St. Catherine's, Ontario to Irish immigrant parents on April 1, 1859. Growing up in Buffalo's hard scrapple "First Ward" district, he joined the ranks of countless other Sons of Erin who worked the docks and eventually was trained to become an iron worker. Dissatisfied by the tedium of those professions, Michael, who enjoyed theatrical performances, decided at the age of 23 to try his hand at the world of entertainment. While so many hopefuls longed to grace the stage, it was Michael's ambition to own them.

From 1890 to 1913, he successfully operated several theaters and music halls on both sides of the Niagara River. Later, with silent films growing in popularity, he opened the Hippodrome Theater in 1914 which was one of the region's first venues dedicated to that entertainment genre. As his success grew so did his dreams and ambitions. Shea's next logical move was to build a new type of theater, one that would become a regional showcase. He wished to combine the worlds of the silver screen and live vaudeville performances on an opulent scale. With this vision in mind, Michael Shea would settle for nothing less than spectacular.

Billed as "The Wonder Theater" when it was opened in January of 1926, Shea's Buffalo Theater quickly became the flagship of Michael's theatrical empire. This eight-story, terra cotta-trimmed building was designed by Cornelius and George Rapp who were renowned for their work on other theatric palaces and was built at a cost of approximately $2,000,000. Its interior was created to resemble the opera houses of sixteenth and seventeenth century Europe and is considered a fine example of recreated Spanish, French Baroque, and Rococo styles. The grand staircase was lined with polished marble, mirrors, and completed with a beautiful crystal chandelier. So opulent was this theater that the advanced opening night publicity stated:

THERE'S ROOM FOR ALL
WE'VE MADE THIS THEATRE TREMENDOUS IN SIZE
AS WELL AS OVERWHELMINGLY MAGNIFICENT IN DECORATION
IT WILL HUSH YOU, AWE YOU, STAGGER YOU —
AN ACRE OF SEATS
THE MIGHTIEST SIGHT WITHIN FOUR WALLS
IN ALL AMERICA WILL BURST UPON YOU WHEN
YOU STEP INSIDE OUR COLOSSAL NEW THEATRE

To complete this theatrical marvel, a Wurlitzer pipe organ was installed as well as a radical new innovation called "air conditioning," making it one of the very first theaters in the nation to be so equipped.

As the city's population began their exodus to the suburbs, "Shea's Buffalo" suffered declining attendance causing it to change ownership many times. Eventually, it was sold to the City of Buffalo through foreclosure and was closed on June 30th, 1975. It was resurrected later that year and tenuously stayed open through 1979. In 1980, the Shea's Preservation Guild was formed to manage the theater, and in February 2000, the building was officially deeded to them. Today, Shea's Theater is on The National Register of Historic Places and enjoys the benefit of being restored by a dedicated staff. It currently maintains an ambitious schedule playing host to many of the luminaries of today's entertainment fields.

While this grande dame of theaters has enjoyed a resurgence in popularity, there are those who many not be of the living variety that climb the grand staircase to its balcony. Many whispered tales have been uttered amongst the building's employees. Once, during the rehearsal of the hit musical "Beauty and the Beast," a member of the cleaning staff was startled when the phrase, "Isn't it wonderful," was clearly heard. Turning quickly, a distinguished gentleman dressed in a gray flannel suit was briefly seen. Could this be the same man who has been reported occupying Mr. Shea's personal seat located in the balcony? The most recent sighting occurred in 2000 as renovation work was being conducted. A member of the volunteer preservation staff saw a "well-dressed man" who said to her, "Isn't it magnificent?" With that she turned and saw the man quickly disappear. Later, she identified this apparition as being that of Michael Shea whose portrait now hangs in the theater.

In July of 2006, I was an Associate Pastor of a small Spiritualist Church in Niagara Falls, New York. We had received a gracious invitation to do an investigative "walk through" and tour of this historic and paranormally active theater. Arriving at the location I was struck with how beautiful this building actually was amid a decaying urban backdrop. As a medium, the feeling of residual energy was the first impression that I received. This was probably caused by the multitude of theater patrons who had passed through it doors over its many decades of existence. As we entered the lobby and met our tour guides, I subjectively received the impressions of men and women dressed in 1950s clothing, walking in a large group down the main staircase. At this point, we attempted to check EMF readings, however they proved to be extremely high due to all of the electrical lines and lights that were in use throughout the building. This would render our EMF meters totally useless.

Climbing the grand staircase and stopping at the landing, the vibrations of a spirit child with brunette hair and dressed in a slightly soiled blouse and jumper became apparent. As I continued up the stairs, I became aware of what is known as a "trace" or the path that the entity most probably used to move from one area to another. This

Shea's Theater.

type of energy signature is sometimes found in intelligent hauntings as the movement of spirit energy will leave a sort of pattern as the spirit personalities move to different locations at regular intervals. Delving a bit deeper into the life of the child, I was told by my spirit guides that she had passed from this life between the ages of 8 and 10 from a possible lung problem and that it was in this place that she had spent her most happiest moments.

Reaching the lower area of the balcony and looking towards the stage, I sensed that two spirit workmen were standing to the left side of the orchestra pit. Both wore common "mechanic's hats" of the early 1900s and what appeared to be bib overhauls. The images that were shown to me seemed to indicate that one spirit worker was dissatisfied about something, demonstrating this by placing his hands on his hips while shaking his head. At the time of the "walk through," there was some pre-production work for an upcoming play going on. Could this be the reason for the spectral workman's dismay?

Our guide next showed us a mirror that was located in a women's restroom. This was no ordinary dressing room mirror as it occupied almost the entire wall and was literally floor to ceiling in height. There was something unusual and I perceived it to have a possible psychic "attachment" to it. Impressions of a middle-aged man associated with the mirror flowed into my mind. The best way that I could describe him would have been someone who hid behind it, only "peeking" out on occasion. While I sensed no intentions of impropriety, I did convey to my spirit guides that it was totally inappropriate for him to be there. When I mentioned this fact to our tour guide, I was told that the mirror was brought in from another location which makes sense as I felt that it did not belong there. Hopefully, this spirit will someday realize that he is not bound to the mirror and will go on.

One cannot truly appreciate a building of this magnitude unless you are granted almost total access to it. Unfortunately, while our tour guides did allow us to wander within each area shown to us, no one observed any other any other paranormal phenomena. Nonetheless, it was an overwhelming experience just the same.

When Michael Shea died in 1934, he left behind a legacy that lives on to this day. To say that he, as well as others, may walk upon those carpeted halls can be conceptually proven as fact. If we measure a man by his achievements, then Michael Shea in the form of a memory has created a residual vibration that resonates strongly within that building. He loved his creation, and whenever one looks at the grandeur of this place, Michael Shea is a minute part of everything there. To some this is truly considered immortality.

Chapter 9

Forgotten Tunnels, Ghosts, and the Town Ball Room

Today's modern city has been built upon the ashes of another time. Attempting to explore this past can become a nightmare even for the most jaded of paper chasers. Public records are often found to be incomplete, reference books have been misplaced, and the memories of an elder generation grows faded with time. Unfortunately, much of the information that is needed to provide clues as to why a location is haunted gets lost in the shuffle. The City of Buffalo has many buildings that can defy even the most diligent of researchers. One such enigma is the Town Ballroom.

The Town Ballroom

This nightclub is located on Main Street and its current owners believe that the building may have been the site of a carriage repair shop and livery stable. Paranormal Researcher Rob Lockhart has been able to trace it origins as far back as the 1870s when it was used as a warehouse for W.H. Glenny, Sons & Co., one of the largest import houses in the nation. Perhaps the most interesting period of occupancy for this building came during Prohibition when it was a restaurant called the Town Supper Club (changed later to the Town Casino). Rumors abound that this was a speakeasy for the well-heeled classes of Buffalo. Also, this may have been where the notorious gangster, Al Capone, visited when he was in town to check on local operations. It is said that "Scarface" was often seen playing high stakes poker in the basement. This does make sense as Buffalo was an important port on the Great Lakes and had easy access to Canada. Of interest, too, is the now bricked-up entrance to the mostly forgotten Buffalo tunnel system. These tunnels may have been used to store and transport illegal goods and alcohol.

With its somewhat checkered past The Town Ballroom cannot help but have its share of paranormal activity. A few years ago when it was doing business under the name "Sphere" employees would report that they heard the sounds of doors slamming and heavy footsteps while they worked in the basement. Also, there was a strong feeling of being watched or having someone standing directly behind them when no one else was there. The catwalk located behind the stage is said to be active and regularly hosts spectral roadies that may help the living ones tear down after an evening's performance. Cold spots have been encountered while the sounds of a party in full swing can be heard even though the popular nightspot was closed. Perhaps the most unnerving experience has been the sighting of an elegant-looking Victorian woman possessing blond hair, who wore a cream-colored, satin dress. She has been seen by a former manager in the club's liquor storage room.

It seems that some of the phantom party goers will occasionally reach out and touch people. Paranormal Investigator Sandra Barnes had just such an experience.

The Town Ballroom.

In 2003, while she was doing a "walk through" in the area behind the stage, she felt "a hand lay flat on her right shoulder." She relates that it was never a threatening "touch," but instead felt like a "reassuring" hand....almost as if saying "this is mine" (in regards to the building). Sandra immediately looked and realized that no one was around. It was then that she heard a "breath" in her left ear.

In January of 2007, I was invited to take part in an event at The Town Ballroom called "Lifting The Curse" which entailed an evening of talks on paranormal topics, psychic readings, and just shaking off the winter doldrums. One of the public activities planned was a guided tour of the building's "haunted basement." I will attest to the fact that merely entering into this underground maze of rooms and passages can be quite disorientating. As I walked behind our tour guide, I began to notice a slight tingling sensation on my arms. Checking with my own EMF meter, I found that many of these passages did indeed have extremely high levels of EMF. Immediately, I began to look for a source and found that in the older sections of the basement, the walls in some spots were literally lined with electrical conduits and breaker boxes. Paranormal Investigators refer to this type of location as a "Fear Cage" because of the high EMF levels that are often associated with it. Studies have shown that repeated or prolonged exposure to such levels can cause anything from feelings of being watched, fear, hallucinations, skin rashes, to certain types of cancers. This would also explain why some employees who have experienced prolonged exposure to this EMF source were privy to so many claims of paranormal activity associated with this building. However, because of the numerous personal experiences that have been collected over the years, there still may be a more ghostly cause.

The Forgotten Tunnels

In most major cities, we find that an underground system of tunnels have been created to facilitate the movement of goods as well as providing access for power and support services needed to operate a modern-day metropolis. Over time, many of these tunnels have fallen into disrepair and lie mostly forgotten under the modern streets of the city. Today in Buffalo, only a handful of municipal workers and a few urban explorers know of their existence. With the passage of time these "vaults," as they are sometimes called, are starting to become structurally weakened by the constant bombardment of heavy traffic. One such tunnel was rediscovered in September of 2008 when the sidewalk that borders Washington Street collapsed near the former AM&A's buildings. The tunnels run beneath the street and were used to move merchandise from one building to another. We also know that these spaces were sometimes used by employees because when the roof of this particular tunnel collapsed, lockers could be easily seen when you looked down into the sinkholes. While many locations for these tunnels are lost to time, you still can identify a few by looking for metal street curbs. Those are sure indications that there may be something under the current urban sidewalks.

The Town Ballroom and its underground world have a long and interesting history. Its haunted reputation is probably only enhanced by such a past. But still the question remains, is the building and tunnel entrance haunted? I believe that they are, but to what extent is for others to decide.

Chapter 10

The Specter of Death and the Angels of Mercy

The German Roman Catholic Orphanage

When the Industrial Revolution came to western New York, it was considered by many historians to have been a double-edged sword. With the rapid growth of industry came an influx of workers needed to man the docks and factories of the burgeoning port city. However, with this increased population came devastating urban maladies that were caused by a lack of proper sanitation, poor hygiene, and adequate housing. Many illnesses that we no longer think of as common swept through the region leaving in their wake suffering that this nation has not experienced in generations. But for those who became infected during the dreaded cholera epidemics that ravaged Buffalo from 1849 through 1851, death may have been a welcomed relief.

Close-knit neighborhoods who shared food and water supplies soon fell prey to cholera. So deadly was this disease that a person within forty-eight hours of becoming infected would begin to suffer from vomiting and watery diarrhea to the extent that they would rapidly lose enough bodily fluids to induce extreme dehydration, shock, as well as becoming comatose. Once in a coma, the specter of death would not be far behind. The local medical community relying upon archaic treatments were rendered impotent by this disease.

With the increasing death rate, there rose among the city's population a rising number of orphaned children. During this era, publicly funded social services were virtually non existent. Any aid for these waifs for the most part came from charities and the religious sector. Orphanages and a network of occupational training facilities slowly emerged to save the children from the claws of degradation, poverty, and despair.

One such orphanage was founded in 1852 by Reverend Joseph Helmpraecht, who was the pastor of St. Mary's Church. He began to notice that there were many children living in the homes of the parish's sick and destitute. These he would bring back with him and provide for their care until a parishioner would take them in. It became quickly apparent that the need far outweighed the church's resources and it was decided that something had to be done. Initially, the Sisters of St. Francis were chosen to shoulder the responsibility of the care of children until the age of 10 at a small orphanage that had been constructed next to their convent in Batavia, New York.

In order to fund this operation, Rev. Helmpraecht's successor, Rev. Urbanczick, asked each parishioner of St. Mary's to donate twenty-five cents quarterly to keep the home running. When financial concerns grew to the critical stage, nine German Catholic parishes joined together to develop a plan to meet an ever-growing need and incorporated as an orphans asylum in 1874. A site was chosen on Dodge Street, but before construction could begin there was a major obstacle. The newly purchased land was an old Catholic burial ground. The remains had to be exhumed and were "transferred" to a mass grave at Mt. Calvary Cemetery, being marked by a single stone.

The orphanage's cornerstone was laid on November 1st, 1874, and it opened its doors on June 6th, 1875. The German Catholic Orphanage was described as a three-story, brick building, with a basement, two wings, running water, and gas lights, on a seventeen-acre campus that boasted a vegetable garden, cow pastures, and a playground. A fire swept through the Orphanage on Ash Wednesday, March 5, 1919, causing $150,000 in damages. Within six months, a new and improved facility was built. In 1938, work was begun on the Sacred Heart Chapel as well as a connecting passageway to the main building. By 1950, a hospital, laundry room, auditorium, and pool had been added. Eventually, with a dwindling orphan population, the structure was converted to a Diocesan Preparatory Seminary and then later to the Diocesan Educational Campus. Finally in the 1990s, the school was closed and sold to private developers and fell into its current state of disrepair.

In 2008, I struck up a conversation with paranormal investigator and historic preservationist John Crocitto while attending a social function at the Iron Island Museum. Interestingly, our conversation eventually turned to the topic of the German Catholic Orphanage and how he had actually been inside the abandoned buildings. John told me about how an accidental meeting with the supervisor of a work detail mowing grass at the site had enabled him to enter the buildings and conduct a paranormal investigative "walk through."

Walking through the shattered glass doors of the entrance, John immediately noticed several cold spots and what sounded to him as desks being dragged and dropped. Following the sounds, he was brought to a room where desks were indeed present and strewn haphazardly about. This was most likely caused by the rampant vandalism that these buildings are subjected to but did not explain the source of the sounds.

The German Roman Catholic Orphanage Chapel.

Making his way to the former boy's dormitory, he experienced two very loud bangs against the walls which caused him to search for an intruder, however, no one was found.. Startled but intrigued, he conducted an EVP session from which produced the voice of a little boy saying, "lead the way" and a very "hoarse cough." Also captured in that location was an adult female who said, "I can't find you." Further exploring the dormitory, John witnessed what seemed to be the form of a small child peeking from the darkened hallway. The pointing of his flashlight's beam found the hall devoid of human company.

Continuing his exploration, he began to investigate what used to be the girl's dormitory. John remembered feeling uneasy as if someone was watching him. Conducting his next EVP session, he recorded a sort of rhythmic humming that sounded as if done by the voice of a young girl. Also, while slightly challenging any possible entities during this session, he joked, "I eat little children for breakfast." When he played back the recording, he immediately heard following his comment, "Dream On," in an unmistakable girl's voice.

Perhaps the most impressive but foreboding building left on the grounds is the chapel. Entering into the former place of worship, John found the floor strewn with old hymnals, walls covered by graffiti, a moldering organ, and a broken statue of Christ crucified upon the cross giving it a hellish atmosphere. Making his way through the debris to an area near the confessionals, he began to hear audibly what seemed to be whispers. This could not have been the worker mowing the grass as they were located at another area. They were loud enough to be described as being a conversation yet too soft to be understood.

The Original Orphanage Building.

While all of John's experiences are of interest, perhaps the one that most peaked my attention had to do with the moving of the original burial grounds. As he began to record himself talking about the subject and the remains that were moved, there came a reply on his voice recorder, "It's only a monument." This response may be in reference to the single monument that was placed at the mass grave in Mount Calvary Cemetery where the remains were reburied.

The circumstances that caused the German Catholic Orphanage to be built in the first place were indeed heart wrenching. Is there nothing more pitiful than the plight of orphaned or destitute children? The question does however remain, are there spirits who still reside within this abandoned facility? To John Crocitto, who walked those halls alone, there is absolutely no doubt that they do.

Chapter 11

Iron Rails and Not So Silent Spirits

The Buffalo Central Terminal

The Buffalo Central Terminal has dominated the skyline of the city's East Side since its completion in 1929. Rising above the neighborhood's rooftops, this seventeen-story building is a fine example of the Art Deco-style popular in the 1920s. Designed by the architectural firm of Fellheimer & Wagner for the New York Central Railroad, it was constructed at the cost of $14 million dollars. The main terminal concourse is an impressive 225 feet in length, 66 feet wide, and 58.5 feet high. The tower, which has an observation deck, soars 15 stories and can be seen for miles. Inside this impressive structure were housed various shops, offices, a trolley station, underground cab garage, waiting rooms, and a very large restaurant. None who entered this train terminal during its heyday could ever forget its grandeur and beauty.

With the Japanese attack on Pearl Harbor and the United States entry into World War II, rail travel gained in popularity. With so many servicemen and women passing through the doors of the terminal a USO Cantina was set up on the mezzanine level that overlooks the main concourse. As a gesture for good luck departing servicemen walking towards the platforms would often touch the hooves of a stuffed bison that had been placed on display as a symbol of municipal pride. So many touched the bison that its course hair was almost rubbed bare and eventually had to be replaced by a plaster replica.

The terminal enjoyed a healthy existence throughout the war years, but as it slowly began to end, so did America's love affair with the "Iron Horse." More efficient means of transportation took precedent, namely the automobile and airplane. Suffering from a marked decrease in business, the passenger trains that once regularly stopped at the Buffalo Central Terminal were discontinued in 1979. With the rail industry in a tailspin, Conrail officially closed its offices a year later.

Slowly, the firms who once ran their businesses from the terminal tower relocated elsewhere, and in their absence, only the echoes of a more prosperous time remained.

Attempting to save the building from ruin, Anthony Fedele & Galesi Realty bought it for $75,000. Fedele actually took up residency in the terminal tower for several years where his social gatherings became legendary. The main concourse was then rented out for floor hockey tournaments, dances, and other cultural events. Unfortunately, Fedele went bankrupt and with this came a dark period of neglect and vandalism. The new owners stripped and sold all of the lighting fixtures, central clock, decorative railings, benches, and mail boxes. Local vandals then descended upon the property like vultures ripping the wiring and copper pipes from the walls in order to sell them to scrap dealers. Even its signature plaster bison suffered an insult when it was backed into and badly damaged by a truck driven by careless salvage workers. Security at this time was very lax and more damage was done in the form of graffiti being sprayed upon its once-polished marble walls, fires set, and the breaking of every window in the tower. With no widows to serve as protection from the weather, the interior quickly deteriorated and massive water damage occurred. It seems that the only residents of the battered Buffalo Central Terminal became the transients and drug addicts seeking shelter in its lower levels.

It was not until the 1990s when local preservationists began an asserted effort to save the crumbling structure. With landmark status having already been granted in 1984, the owners saw a way to rid themselves of this huge liability. The terminal was sold for a dollar in 1997 and the property was transferred to the Central Terminal Restoration Corporation.

The Buffalo Central Terminal in 1935 from a post card in the author's collection.

With its Gothic architecture and derelict past, the Buffalo Central Terminal is considered by many urban explorers to be a natural setting for paranormal activity to take place. The actual investigation of a location such as the old terminal can present many challenges. The size of the structure alone is quite daunting. Limited sources of power, lack of ambient light, as well as floors literally covered in papers, mold, fallen plaster, broken glass, asbestos, and other debris adds to a mounting list of concerns. It is because of these issues that public access is not often granted to "closed areas." However, several times during 2009, I was lucky enough to have secured invitations by the terminal's event coordinator, Ryan Willard, to explore its secrets. Ryan is also the co-founder of WNY GhostHunters and it was his paranormal investigative group that volunteered to clean several floors of the tower so that it would become safe enough for visitors to tour during fundraising events.

The phenomena that has been experienced seems to be of a benign nature. A common occurrence found inside of the old train terminal is that of shadow beings. I have personally witnessed several while simply walking along its main concourse. The most striking was seen during the day when a "shadow man" was observed floating just inside the ticket window area. Once spotted it disappeared into the back wall. Also volunteers talk about a man who is often seen walking along the mezzanine level located directly above the ticket booths. He is likely unaware that the entryway which he regularly passes through is now bricked up, giving credence to this ghost being residual in nature.

In addition to shadow people, it seems that this area has become a hotbed for the collection of EVPs. The most impressive evidence of that type has been captured by investigator Jeff Fredericks. Jeff wanted to see if he could get a direct response by asking a question commonly heard at a train ticket booth from a discarnate entity. He asked, "Can I have a ticket to Chicago? Almost immediately the reply, "Of course, quarters please," is heard on the recording. Was this an intelligent entity who now resides in a parallel dimension or the residual response to an often asked question? EVP captures at the terminal have amounted to the bulk of the evidence found. Another good example of an EVP was collected on what is now called the Fedele floor, where the former owner's apartment was once located. It is thought by many to be the voice of a young boy saying, "They call me Zachary." Who he is and why he would be associated in this area, no one really knows.

Opposite page: The Buffalo Central Terminal in 2010.

Paranormal activity has been reported occurring on almost every floor and hallway on the property. Photographs taken on the third and fourth floors show a moving, bluish orb. Disembodied voices have been heard as well as the sighting of "people" gathered around a long-removed hallway water fountain. The most unnerving of any area within the terminal has to be the underground trolley level. Not only is it physically imposing reminding those lucky enough to explore it of a cavern, but on certain evenings the activity levels seem to become amplified. It was there that I witnessed a "black mass" which seemed to obscure any ambient light. Along with that experience, I also saw the head and shoulders of a shadow being that walked towards us in a subterranean hallway. On a recent investigation, an electronic "Hack Box" session was conducted and the phrase, "Go home," was repeated several times. Apparently, whoever resides down in that dank, dark place resented the intrusion of investigators.

One never knows what you will see or find at the Buffalo Central Terminal. As I was exploring near some deteriorating boxes, I found a very stylized "talking board." It was probably left behind by a low-budget movie production crew who filmed there often—an interesting relic to be left behind in a very haunted location.

Opposite page: Ryan Willard of WNY Ghosthunters setting up an IR Camera.

Ryan Willard and Brandon Bristol investigating the entrance to the Underground Trolley Level.

Probably the most unique tool that is currently being used by the paranormal community for spirit communication is the ordinary flashlight. It has become popular because of its simplicity and relatively inexpensive cost. The theory behind this experiment is that spirits can manipulate just enough energy to create a slight pressure on the lens housing which allows the light switch to on or off. (The manufacturer when contacted about any possible reason for this phenomena has said that outside of massive switch corrosion, what is happening, simply should not.) This type of communication has been used with great success at the terminal and is believed to have aided spirits to bridge the gap between the ethers.

This stone, steel, and concrete landmark has witnessed many changes over its lifetime. Once it was part of a vibrant neighborhood teaming with well kept homes, churches, and shops. It is unfortunate that the Buffalo Central Terminal, formerly an important hub of transportation has now become seen as a neglected and decaying hulk. However, with a new sense of purpose given to it by preservationists, it will begin to enjoy a new life. To the dedicated people

The Main Concourse.

A Talking Board found in the Trolley Level in a debris pile.

who love this building, it has become a symbol of victory and renewal for the City of Buffalo. For those who silently walk along its darkened halls, it is simply home.

A Love Triangle At The Trestle

The railroad with all of its accompanying industrial arteries was extremely important to the fabric of Buffalo and its neighboring communities. Perhaps the most important trains that traveled along the iron highways to western New York were the great "black snakes" which carried freight that fueled the local economy, created jobs, as well as heated the homes of its growing workforce. In an age when the use of natural gas was not wide spread, coal was indeed king.

Located along Union Road, near the Conrail overpass and next to the Town of Cheektowaga Highway Department stands three lone relics of a bygone age. These monolithic concrete support columns are all that remain of one of the regions largest coal trestles. This structure was needed to transfer coal from arriving rail cars to waiting delivery wagons. Small "hopper cars" filled with coal were pushed up the trestle by a "switch engine" to its second story. Underneath a wagon would be waiting for the "chute" doors of the trestle to open, filling it with anthracite.

Owned by Jake Kluczycki, the trestle was an impressive achievement for the hard-working Polish immigrant. The long hours spent at the trestle afforded him little time for a social life. As his business grew, so did Jake's need for companionship. His search for a suitable wife was complete when he met Paula, a woman barely out of her twenties and less than half his age. He wooed her with expensive gifts, married her, and with no time for a honeymoon, they began their life together working at the trestle.

At the turn of the 1900s, the City of Buffalo found itself in the midst of a building boom. It was a crown jewel among the cities of the Great Lakes and a celebration of that prosperous time would be showcased at the upcoming Pan American Exhibition. More coal would be needed to fuel the furnaces of homes and industry in this thriving community.

One evening at Casey's, a local bar that was located a short distance from the coal trestle, Jake met a guy named Mark who was looking for work. Having run many aspects of the trestle himself over the years, Jake was beginning to feel his age and needed someone who could pull the stiff levers that opened the hopper chutes. Also, as this was a multi - leveled structure, he needed an able-bodied man who could climb the steep ladders and shovel the coal that had fallen from the moving hopper cars. As Mark was young and strong, Jake hired him on the spot.

However, all was not idyllic in the coal yards. Paula at once realized that her dreary days spent working at the trestle seemed lighter when Mark was around. He gave her the attention that her workaholic husband rarely did, which made her feel more like a woman again. Inevitably, the two fell in love and spent their evenings together while Jake concentrated on his business, working late into the night. As time went on, Paula decided that she wanted a divorce from Jake, but Mark was only a poor laborer. Without certain financial support, they would most certainly have had to endure a hard scrapple life. The two lovers needed to hatch a plot to do away with Jake and then, once in control of his estate, could live happily ever after. But how to do it?

Time was of the essence as she knew that Jake realized the demand for coal was beginning to decrease and that the use of natural gas rapidly began to take its place. In fact, he recently had a gas line installed in his office which fueled his own furnace. The crown that coal once possessed now began to slowly slip away. Sensing this future economic downturn, Jake forced the lovers' hand when he announced that: "We are going to sell [the trestle and] move back to Poland, you will like it there with my family." Unhappy at the prospect of going to a foreign land and losing Mark forever, it was decided that something drastic and immediate had to be done.

It is at this point where the legend of the coal trestle grows somewhat vague. Some western New York railway enthusiasts who were interviewed for this story say that Mark and Paula sabotaged the building, and when it collapsed, the newly installed gas line exploded killing all three. In an another account, Jake caught wind of the plot, and in a rage, killed Mark and Paula, hiding the evidence and their bodies in the great piles of coal. Jake then packed his belonging and escaped to his native land. Regardless of which ending you prefer, there sprang from this tragic love triangle a ghost story that has endured to this very day.

It is said that on the anniversary of Paula's death, she is seen wandering the ruined concrete supports of this once mighty trestle searching for her beloved Mark. Ghost lights are often seen flickering in the area. Those who venture to the site also feel as if they are being watched by unseen eyes. Local teens regularly sneak over the tracks [the site is located on Conrail property which is private] and explore the ruins when the moon is full. Recently, several paranormal investigators have visited the area and report that they monitored several floating EMF spikes between the first and second supports where it is said that the office once stood.

Little is left of this once-proud trestle. Nature is slowly reclaiming it and the mighty concrete supports wither with each passing year. Alone it stands as a monument to one man's ambition as well as how easy it is to lose sight of the important things in life, one of which being love.

Another view of The Old Coal Trestle.

Remains of the former Coal Trestle.

Chapter 12

The Keepers of Memories

The Buffalo Museum of Science

Designed by August Esenwein and James A. Johnson, The Buffalo Museum of Science first opened its doors on January 19, 1929. This impressive building houses a world-class collection of botanical, geological, fossil, insect, animal, as well as anthropological specimens.

The museum can trace its origins back to 1836 when the Young Men's Association was founded in the City of Buffalo. The YMA was a public organization that administered to the city's cultural and scientific endeavors. In the process, this organization acquired an impressive collection of fossils, minerals, insects, pressed plants, paintings, as well as other specimens and historic relics. As the collection grew, so did the need for proper display space. In 1861, The Buffalo Society of Natural Sciences was formed and it was decided that a permanent building should be erected to house and display its collections.

The Buffalo Museum of Natural Sciences.

Over the years many visitors as well as staff and workmen have experienced a variety of supernatural encounters. One incident is the sighting of a ghostly male often seen walking after hours in the area of Hamlin Hall (which is known as the main exhibition hall). Staff members believe that it may be the apparition of Chauncey Hamlin who had been elected the museum's president in 1920.

During another paranormal sighting, "shadowy beings" were reportedly witnessed by security guards one evening as the entities seemingly floated out from the "When Ankh: The Circle Of Life In Ancient Egypt" exhibition. This area is thoroughly covered by security cameras, and when reviewed, the tapes revealed nothing out of the ordinary. Could these wandering "shadows" be the restless spirits of those mummified remains now on display?

More recently a variety of experiences have been reported. Mysterious sounds, whispers, and footsteps have all been heard in the hallways of the Anthropology Department. A former staff member tells that once while working alone in that area she saw the pacing "shadow" of someone or something that was visible under the door of the main collections area. Not having the keys, she prudently decided not to have security open it and left whomever was in there to their own spectral business. On another occasion after leaving an office, the blinds would be found open, seemingly by themselves when she returned. Also, doorknobs in that same location were seen moving with no one on the other side of the door.

This same staffer also reported that she witnessed a full-bodied apparition that stood near a hall corner. The entity was visible for only a few seconds, but long enough for her to see that this ghostly visitor was a male, wore a suit, and had short hair. What is interesting is that she saw him at 9am in the morning proving that paranormal phenomena can happen at anytime of the day or night.

Not to be outdone by her spectral male counterparts, a phantom woman attired in an "antique red dress" walks near the public area known as the "Connections." In that same location, volunteers and staff members have heard what sounds like someone who was "wearing sneakers and running on pavement." The odd thing is that the floors in that area are all carpeted. Perhaps this is a question of two overlapping dimensions—are two spirits from different time periods inhabiting the same space?

From the many reports received, one may assume that the Buffalo Museum of Science is a haven for playful, intelligent spirits. However, if we take into consideration that objects may hold the emotional signatures of their former owners, perhaps what is being experienced at the museum may be residual in nature. Until someone makes an attempt at communication with any possible spirit personalities that inhabit the building, we shall have to be content to let those who encounter such phenomenon to decide for themselves. What we do know for certain is that the Buffalo Museum of Science is a vibrant center for learning. Perhaps it is that vibrancy and human interaction that triggers the many dormant objects in its collections to come back to life.

The Iron Island Museum

Tucked neatly away in the city's Lovejoy District, the Iron Island Museum is a reflection of the area's rich railroad heritage. During an age when rail transportation linked Buffalo to the world, this unique neighborhood provided homes for its workers and was literally bordered on all sides by its steel veins of track. It was this feature that gave the area its nickname, the "Iron Island."

The structure that houses the museum was originally built for the Lovejoy Methodist Episcopal Church in 1885 and has experienced many incarnations throughout the subsequent years. In 1956, the congregation sold the building to Ronald Wozniak, a funeral director who extensively remodeled the interior and opened it as a mortuary in 1958. A false ceiling was built which hid the former church's stained-glass windows. New interior walls were added so the open space could be subdivided into "viewing rooms" offices, living quarters, and an embalming room (which was located in the area of the present day kitchen). When the mortuary changed hands, it was eventually sold to Pacer Funeral Homes and then to the Amigone Funeral Homes, Inc., who operated it until its closure in the 2000. Having no use for the building, the owners donated it to the Iron Island Preservation Society of Lovejoy, Inc. for use as a museum which opened in October of 2000.

As the Lovejoy district's past is interwoven with that of the railroads, its unique history is highlighted through many of the museum's artifacts and displays. However, it is the common man who lived and worked within the "island's" confines that is showcased. Most poignant is a small display that contains a few items from a more personal past. Curator Marge Thielman Hastreiter's son, who passed at a young age, was waked from this building and is remembered with a small exhibit. It is no wonder that the structure is so lovingly cared for and important to both the community as well as the Hastreiter family themselves.

Almost from the day that the Society assumed ownership of the building paranormal activity has been reported. Shadow beings, strange sounds, footsteps echoing from the attic, pinpoint floating orbs, apparitions, and odd feelings have been experienced by both visitors and staff members alike. Even a "ghost cat" is seen and heard on a regular basis. Its meow has been captured on EVP recordings.

The Hastreiter family who are the primary curators of the museum have been the ones who seem to experienced much of the phenomena that investigators now search for. Marge who spends the most time in the building has heard her name being called as well as heard many other strange sounds. Her daughter, Linda, has her own tales to tell. She once witnessed a shadow being that resembled a priest wearing a dark veil over what looked like a "mitre" or ritual head piece that is sometimes worn by a bishop. Linda also speaks of a time when she was in the museum alone and heard the sounds of tables and chairs being moved. Upon inspection she found that nothing was moved so she decided to call a friend and wait for her outside.

In 2007, I was invited by paranormal investigator Greg Hoffman to be part of the one of the first teams to investigate the Iron Island Museum. As we entered into the building through the front door, I

The Iron Island Museum.

was immediately greeted by a shadow person approximately five-foot-ten-inches in height that exited the hallway to the left and into a former viewing room. So dense was this mass that it obscured the hall's ambient light. During subsequent visits, this entity has been witnessed several times by investigators.

Along with seeing shadow beings, various raps and bangs can be often heard. Most of theses noises are attributed to the old building itself, however, a few cannot. I have personally held vigils and séances in the museum, and when asked for a sound to be repeated, it often does. This type of phenomena is reminiscent of the type of spirit communication exhibited through the Fox Sisters of Hydesville, New York. Other staff members have reported hearing heavy audible "sighs" which on several occasions have been recorded.

The most common form of evidence captured at the museum are EVPs. After interviewing many of the paranormal teams who have visited the museum, it seems that most do capture these disembodied voices, some having a more humorous side to them. Once when attending a function where I began to sing to Marge, staff member

Paranormal Investigator Greg Hoffman checking for vibrations that are often emanating from the alter.

Sandra Barnes captured an EVP telling me to, "Shut up." It seems that whomever was there at the time was definitely a music critic. Also, for whatever reason, it seems that the voices of children are collected on a regular basis. The entity "Tommy" is often recorded, as well as children calling out the names of investigators.

The Military Room houses artifacts from the neighborhood's participation in several of the world conflicts. EVP evidence has turned up the sounds of gun fire and explosions. Could this be a form of residual energy that may become attached to one of the many artifacts housed there? Emotional attachments to objects can cause this type of phenomena. More research needs to be done to find the answer.

Investigators have also found that the use of "Hack Box" technology can produce very interesting results. I have witnessed on several occasions my name along with other investigators on my team having been broadcast from the box. A more disturbing phenomena that is sometimes reported is the use of obscene language that is heard through this device. The first time that someone experiences this can be a frightening moment, however there are a few schools of thought on this matter. It is possible that something nasty like a lower spirit can be attracted to the scanning device in the attempt to frighten session participants, just as is done with the incorrect use of talking boards. Or could it be that the devise may be picking up on a spirit who in life used rather "salty" language, as many believe that our personalities do not change when we pass to the other side? This could be just that person's way of speaking (and I think that we all know individuals who speak this way). Lastly, it may be that spirits are trying to prove that they are really there. By swearing, the spirit may be attempting to use language that is not accepted by the current rules of the FCC. In my experience, once this language is acknowledged, it stops and spirit communication will begin in earnest. I caution everyone though to be careful when using the "Hack Box" as it is akin to meeting a stranger and bringing him into your home.

Humor can also be conveyed through these means. Recently, I took part in a session where my digital recorder's battery's drained. As I had a problem getting it to work after I changed them, I in jest asked for help from the other side. The response to this query was, "Don't ask." Once the recorder was running again, I said sarcastically, "Thanks for the help," to which the box responded, "Retard." I guess whomever was trying to communicate with us thought little of my rudimentary technical skills.

While solid photographic evidence can be rare at any location, a dark mist is sometimes captured in the museum. I have often witnessed this in the "chapel room" where the former casket showroom was located. Also in this room, there is an alter that came from another former Lovejoy church which seems to have vibrations emanating

The hidden stained-glass windows located in the attic of the museum.
Shadow Beings and Black Masses are often seen in this area.

from it. I placed a motion detector having LED lights that will light up when movement occurs and found that it indeed registered some vibrations. Other investigators have felt this sensation when holding onto the small alter columns.

Perhaps the most interesting of all places in the museum is the attic where the false ceiling has hidden the old stained-glass windows. It was there during the taping of a television show that a black mass rushed towards the investigator who was standing on a ladder. This movement caused him to almost slip from the rung on which he stood. A medium who conducted a walk through of the museum said that this ghost's name was "Edgar" and it was he who wished to be left alone up there. During another investigation a remote IR camera picked up a dark shadow that moved near the camera. Could this be related somehow to the first recorded incident?

Personally, the creepiest place in the building for me is the basement. While I hate these dungeon-like spaces to begin with, this one seems more oppressive than most. The walls are made from field stone and I find it oppressive. Also, to the rear of the basement is a small cramped area where there is only a walkway and the dirt is over waist high on either side. Could this have been some sort of a store room or access to the heating ducts; no one knows. However, I get the most unsettling feeling when I am there. There have been many "sensitives" who have walked into this space and claimed to have felt that there have been burials of children in that location. Frankly, I have never felt such a thing and there is no evidence to support the claim at this time. Probably the most unsettling of the many personal experiences reported by the staff occurred when the Society took possession of the building. Down in the basement were twenty-four containers of human cremains left unclaimed by relatives, one having spilled onto the floor. Could these forgotten souls be those who walk the halls of the Iron Island Museum?

It is through a sense of community pride that the Iron Island District still remains vibrant and alive. Too many times we witness smaller hamlets that somehow become swallowed up into the surrounding communities and in the process lose their history as well as identity. It is through the work of the dedicated volunteers of the Iron Island Preservation Society that these stories will never vanish. As long as there is a neighborhood known as Lovejoy, the Iron Island Museum will be there keeping the history and folklore of the community alive. This building is as vibrant as those who have passed through it doors, as well as a few who perhaps have decided to stay on.

The Buffalo And Erie County Serviceman's Park

"Yesterday, December 7, 1941 – a date which will live on in infamy – the United States of America was suddenly and deliberately attacked by naval and air forces of the Empire of Japan."

~Franklin D. Roosevelt
Address to Congress, December 8, 1941

Listeners were shocked and sickened as they huddled around their radios. The President's speech laid the reality of war at the feet of the nation. An atrocity had occurred. The Unites States would now be forced into a world conflict after the Japanese attack on the naval base at Pearl Harbor, Hawaii.

Immediately, the need to rebuild its mighty armada of warships destroyed in the attack was imperative to the security of the nation. With the building of these vessels, the demand for able and experienced seamen became great. Eventually, the muster rolls of these ships would be filled by young men full of patriot fervor and a desire to revenge those lost at Pearl and captured in the Philippines. Among those who answered the call were five brothers from the sleepy little Midwestern town of Waterloo, Iowa.

Joseph, Francis, Albert, Madison, and George came from a very close knit Irish Catholic family. Just like most boys, they enjoyed attending dances, playing sports, hunting, fishing, and riding motorcycles. In 1937, George and Francis joined the Navy and served four tours of duty returning in 1941. All of the brothers were shaken from their everyday life when news of the attack at Pearl Harbor brought the horrors of war to their doorstep. A friend of George and Francis, Bill Ball from a neighboring town, had been killed and his death spurred all of the brothers to enlist immediately.

The Sullivan boys had a wish that they all serve together onboard the same ship. In the present-day Navy, it is rare that siblings from one family be allowed to do so. However, the brothers were determined and petitioned Washington for an exception to regulations. This request was granted even though Albert at the time had a wife and child on the way. The mood of the brothers was expressed by George when he said, "Well, I guess our minds are made up, aren't they fellows? And when we go in, we want to go in together. And if the worst comes to worst, why we'll have all gone down together." On January 3rd, 1942 they were sworn into service. After receiving instruction at the Great Lakes Naval Training Station, they were assigned to serve aboard the light cruiser USS *Juneau* and sailed for the action in the Pacific.

War is a hellish affair. In the early hours of November 13th 1942, the nightmare battle for Guadalcanal was begun. During the opening

The USS *Sullivans.*

engagements, the *Juneau* was struck by a torpedo fired from the Japanese destroyer *Amatsukaze*. She suffered heavy damage but was able to make sufficient repairs as to get underway and attempt to return to the port at Espiritu Santo for repairs. Later that same day, the wounded vessel began to cross an area referred to by fleet navigators as "Torpedo Alley," a place where enemy submarines would lie in wait for damaged ships. The *Juneau* was targeted and attacked by the Japanese submarine *I-26*. Torpedoes were once again fired and the *Juneau's* magazine exploded, splitting the ship in two. A sailor aboard the nearby USS *Helena* recalled how devastating the explosion was: "I was below decks when she [USS *Juneau*] blew but I came up and the guys told me the [*Juneau's*] forward turret went right over our bow... intact!"

It was said that there may have been at least 100 survivors, but because the fear of another attack was so great, the remaining convoy continued on without launching rescue attempts. When the help finally reached the area, only ten crew members had survived, none bearing the Sullivan surname.

To honor the heroism of the Sullivan brothers, two destroyers have been built and commissioned by the US Navy. The first originally launched on April 4th, 1943, was decommissioned after World War II and brought back into service during the Korean Conflict. After it was decommissioned for a final time, a second ship bearing the Sullivan's name was launched in 1995, and as of this writing, is still in active service.

In one of the great ironies of the tragic saga of the Sullivan's, the Japanese warship that had done the initial damage to the *Juneau*, the *Amatsukaze* was targeted and sunk by the submarine USS *Croaker*. Today the *Croaker* is currently berthed at the Buffalo and Erie County Serviceman's Park alongside the retired destroyer that honorably bears the name USS *Sullivans*. It is a proper place for this avenging angel to spend her retirement years.

Spectral Activity at the Buffalo And Erie County Serviceman's Park

The spectral warships now moored at the Serviceman's Park all seem to share common supernatural threads. The sounds of doors slamming, footsteps, phantom sailors, as well as low whispers have been reported on board all three. However, it is the USS *Sullivans,* that garners much of the attention of the paranormal community. It is specifically said that the Sullivan brothers walk the corridors of their namesake. Dark mists appear in photographs, cold spots are felt, battery drains are very commonly reported at amidships and the apparition of George Sullivan has been

The USS *Croaker.*

seen near the memorial to him and his brothers. Also, many tourists have reported witnessing a man dressed in the garb of a WWII sailor, often leaving berths and the seaman's mess just ahead of them. Thinking that he is a volunteer or tour guide, they attempt to catch up in order to ask a question, but he can never be found.

In the Spring of 2008, I was asked to participate in an investigation of the USS *Sullivans* by WNY Unexplained Paranormal. Almost immediately after our safety briefing by the Chief Engineer, we found out that conducting an investigation aboard a ship does present some problems that you do not normally face while at dry land locations. After performing our pre-investigation "walk through," we quickly realized that power cables laced throughout the vessel rendered our EMF and K-2 meters practically useless. This being the case, it was decided that only camera's, digital recorders, and dowsing rods were going to be used.

Our investigation began in the seamen's mess on the lower deck. I took six photographs with my digital camera and found the new batteries that I had just installed swiftly drained. Within a few minutes of my camera problems, an audible "mid range" tapping sound was heard by the investigators present. As the ship is made of metal, we had to decipher what may have been naturally occurring and what might be a spirit possibly trying to communicate with us. After listening to the sound intently, it was decided that we find the source of the tappings in an attempt to debunk it. Walking through the lower deck and the individual seamen's berths, we realized that the sounds always seemed to be one room in front of us, but never behind us when checked. Eventually, the tapping led us to a ladder from which a slightly louder tapping was now heard. Once up the ladder, we searched for the source and realized that it was coming from a location down a narrow a corridor leading to the Chief Petty Officers mess. Once in this very cramped room, the tapping ceased. An EVP session was undertaken where very low whispers were captured. Several investigators also described the atmosphere in the room as feeling "heavy or thick." Finishing the session, we joked that whomever it was that made the tapping sounds had enjoyed taking us on a tour of his ship.

As we could not use our K-2 meters, I wished to conduct a spirit communication session through the use of dowsing rods. Almost immediately a strong reaction was exhibited to a few basic test questions. The information that was received through this manner seemed to validate that the entity present was indeed a sailor who had served aboard the USS *Sullivans*, but was not one of the brothers who perished on the *Juneau*. Although we could not get his name, he did relate that he was a chief petty officer, served during the Korean War, and that he choose to stay with the vessel as it meant so much to him in life. In retrospect, I find this totally in character with those men whose loyalty to their comrades in arms has survived their mortal passing. A poignant example of this

The Crew's Mess where tapping sounds were heard.

devotion today are the last wishes of many survivors of the attack on Pearl Harbor. As their rolls thin, it is their desire to have their ashes placed aboard the sunken warships that still entomb so many of those brave naval heroes whom rest there.

Concluding the investigation after four cold hours on board the unheated ship, we spoke with the Chief Engineer who related that much of the activity did in fact center in and around the Chief Petty Officer's Mess. That was the location where the most sightings of the phantom sailor have occurred and where visitors seem to feel most uneasy. Also, many staff members and park volunteers when on work details have reported hearing voices from that area when no one else in on board.

So is the USS *Sullivans* haunted? I would have to say that there is a strong intelligent presence that remains attached to the ship. It welcomes those who visit and honor the memory of those who served on her, were rescued by her, and are memorialized by her proud tradition and name.

The Chief Petty Officer's Mess where apparitions have been witnessed.

While I believe that the Sullivan boys themselves are at rest, there is at least one sailor who remains on duty, serving as in life with honor and devotion.

The Alden Public Library

For the residents of this sleepy little town, the local library has always been a place where generations of families could spend countless hours researching childhood school projects or experiencing the joy of reading the latest novel found on the best sellers list. While many of the living come to learn, there is the possibility that a few "spectral visitors" may have stopped by and lingered on.

This impressive gray-stone building is located on Broadway Street which was once the main road that connected Buffalo to all points east. Many years before the Town of Alden was incorporated, this locale was

The Alden Library.

originally known as "lot 17" of the Holland Land Grant. The tract was purchased by Thomas Farnsworth and eventually used as an orchard. The Farnsworths had a daughter named Carrie who eventually married a dashing Union Army Colonel named Joseph Ewell in 1863. Returning after the War of the Rebellion, the Colonel quickly became one of the area's leading citizens. As a member of the Grand Army of the Potomac, an organization made up of Union military veterans, he possessed a lot of political clout and became a leading citizen. Carrie and Colonel Ewell had a daughter whom they named Florence. The child has been described as possessing an inquisitive mind, a love of books, and was an avid reader. Unfortunately, Florence passed from this life in 1906, much to the anguish of her parents and friends.

Soon after Florence's passing, Colonel Ewell's advisors suggested that he make a gift to the people of the Alden area by donating land for public use. A strong supporter of his religion, Joseph gave a portion of the former Farnsworth holdings for the construction of the Stone Presbyterian Church as well as a library which is situated next door. The library was completed in 1913 and dedicated to the memory of Florence in 1914. Over its many years of existence, it has served a variety of purposes including a town meeting hall.

It has been reported that there has been a lot of unusual activity in the library. Its staff has heard whispers, various types of rappings, knockings, and footsteps. Also, some tell of smelling cigar smoke in a stairwell, witnessing an elevator that seemingly has a mind of its own, and the wanderings of a shadow being in the basement hallway which eventually caused a construction worker to leave the building and come back the next day when it was light.

In the late summer of 2009, Glenn and Michelle White contacted the Alden library for permission to conduct a paranormal investigation there. After receiving the needed consent they assembled a team of investigators, myself included, who visited the library several times in the attempt to validate the experiences of the employees. During these investigations, the building was wired with IR surveillance cameras as well as digital video recorders. Motion detectors were placed along the rear corridor leading to the elevator, digital voice recorders were positioned near the stairwell leading down to the basement, as well as a table top motion sensor place on a table in the AV room. Individual team members were equipped with K-2 meters, small flashlights, and personal recorders wherever they went in case the activity may have been localized.

One of the most common pieces of evidence found at haunted sites are those of disembodies voices captured on recording devices. Oftentimes, only the sounds of heavy or labored breathing is heard. EVP captures at the library revealed those as well as other interesting results. Investigators captured the phrase, "Go to Hell," which may have been that of a now-deceased janitor, a voice of a child saying "Mom" was recorded near the Children's Reading Room, and "Caught you here" was captured in the Computer Room. Interesting enough, we find that spirits sometimes have a sense of humor and when one investigator stumbled, the phrase, "Are you drunk?" can be heard.

Working with the team as a medium, I sensed several occurrences that had been previously reported by the library staff. Without prior knowledge given to me, I felt that the spirits who were in this location were there "in visitation" and had wanted to be there.

Also, I could not help but feel that there was a strong "feeling" that these entities may have been hiding in an area of the upper attic or crawlspace. This is a very common phenomena found at similar haunted locations. It seems that ghosts, like some people would rather stay hidden and undisturbed when those of flesh and blood enter their immediate area.

Next, we were taken to the basement where I felt that an entity walked through the central hallway of that area. This was also validated by stories given to investigators by the library's staff. There was also an immediate "energy pull" to the side stairwell where the smell of cigar smoke was reported. Strangely, it was in this area that digital recorders seemed to turn off without an explanation. Several investigators reported an unusual interest in that area. After this fact was mentioned during the "reveal" to staff members, it was found that there is an underground stream near to that location. Water is something that is often associated with many haunted locations and underground streams seem to be a conduit for paranormal activity.

During the course of this investigation, team members reported having varied personal experiences. Several heard whispers coming from the first floor. Flashlights when placed on tables would turn on and off, seemingly indicating *yes* and *no* answers to questions asked. In many instances, K-2 meters registered "hits" in sync with these flashlights. Also, the team witnessed the motion detector that had been placed near the elevator corridor turn on with no one near it. Subsequent efforts to debunk this phenomena could not give investigators any reasonable explanation.

Several times, vibrations on a heavy wooden table that had been located in the AV Room were felt as the team focused their attention during the course of conducting a vigil. As mentioned earlier, in the Spiritualist tradition, this is a phenomenon that is often associated with spirit communication through what is called "table tipping." This type of communication can come in the form of vibrations, knockings as well as tables actually moving or jumping about. On this evening all who sat at the heavy table felt definite vibrations.

While sitting in the AV room, many of the team visually witnessed a bluish white orb that seemingly looked as if it exploded from the area near the main stairwell. The best description that can be used is that of a softball, that was self illuminated, showed brief movement with a trail, and was bright enough for several team members. "Objective Light Anomalies" or visual phenomenon that is experienced by more then two people are extremely rare in the pursuit of paranormal evidence. Immediately this phenomena was investigated and nothing was found as a possible source of the light.

A vigil was next undertaken in the Children's Reading Room, located in the basement. This produced audible whispers, slight knockings, and footsteps again heard by most of the team members. Small pinpoint orbs were observed, one actually seen going into the leg of a team member. During this phase of the investigation, a "shadow person" was seen peering in from the hallway near the door of the room.

All ghostly occurrences do not always happen when there are people around. An interesting event occurred over the weekend after a follow up investigation. When opening the library on Monday morning, a book was found tossed on the floor of the corridor that leads to the elevator. The building, after the subsequent investigations, had been checked by library staff and no stray book would have been left is so obvious a place. Could this be a new mystery that will earn the works of such authors as Edgar Allen Poe or Stephen King?

A library is a repository of learning. It is the keeper of personal experiences and a place where they can be shared with countless individuals. Is there a possibility that a former staff member or even a member of the Ewell family lovingly visits this place? Does the Alden Library possess secrets to share? Is it really haunted? After these investigations, the answer can only be yes.

Chapter 13

Places of Healing

The Haunting Legacy of Father Nelson Baker

Ask anyone who grew up in Buffalo during the 1950s and '60s as to what was the most common threat uttered by frustrated parents and you will hear, "Do that again and you're going to Baker's Orphanage!" It seems that by just invoking the name "Baker" chills could be sent into the heart of the most incorrigible child. Although this threat may have been intimidating, the real "Baker" legacy is one of caring and love.

Nelson Baker was born in Buffalo on February 16th, 1841. His parents ran a grocery store, and from what little is known of his early years, he seems to have enjoyed a normal childhood. When he was old enough, Nelson worked with his brothers in the store and developed a keen interest in bookkeeping. When the Civil War began, Baker joined the 74th Regiment of New York State Militia and was sent in 1863 to guard several important rail passes from Confederate raiders in Pennsylvania. Following the bloody Battle of Gettysburg, the 74th's next duty was to patrol the streets of New York City, following the Draft Riots that had erupted in that city. When he returned to Buffalo at the end of his enlistment, Baker entered into the feed and grain business with his brother, Joseph, which proved to be extremely profitable for a number of years.

In 1869, Baker took a steamer trip that changed his life forever. During periods of prayer and reflection, he felt as if there was a more spiritual path awaiting him. This marked epiphany brought Nelson to enroll at Our Lady of Angels Seminary in preparation for becoming a Catholic priest. Unfortunately, while there he became gravely ill. In December of 1871, he contracted Erysipelas which is a painful infection of the skin and is often fatal. Baker was confined to Sister's Hospital for seventy-seven days, and at one point, was given the Last Rites of Roman Catholic Church. Those who knew him state that his eventual complete recovery was nothing short of miraculous. Returning to the seminary and completing his studies, he was ordained in St. Joseph's Cathedral on March 19th,

Our Lady of Victory Basilica.

Statue of Father Nelson Baker.

1876. The new priest's first assignment was at St. Patrick's Church at Limestone Hill, located in present day Lackawanna, New York. While he was reassigned to a parish in Corning, New York, for a year he returned to St. Patrick's in 1882. The parish was heavily in debt and biographers say that he paid off its creditors out of his own pocket.

Winters in the Buffalo area have always been harsh affairs. The winds that blow over Lake Erie bring with them frigid temperatures and heavy snow falls. Keeping the parish's buildings heated was expensive and Father Baker prayed for relief. Natural Gas had been found in the area, however, deposits were not usually large and drilling for gas was an expensive proposition. Father Baker once again prayed to Our Lady of Victory for help and received a donation of $5,000 from a wealthy member of the parish.

The gas well that Father Baker located for the well drillers.

FATHER BAKER'S GAS WELL

At this site on August 22, 1891 natural gas was found at a depth of 1137 feet. This well and its twin continued to produce sufficient gas for many of the energy needs of Our Lady of Victory Institutions, Basilica, Hospital and Schools. Father Baker's faith caused him to thank Our Lady of Victory for her intercession with God for the gift of the gas from these wells.

When the workers came to the open field where they were to set up their drilling rig, they were met by a procession of clergy, nuns, alter boys, and of course Father Baker praying the rosary. "Where do we dig," they asked? Baker sprinkled the ground with Holy Water and then buried a small statue of the Blessed Virgin. He said, "Dig here, but do not disturb the statue." The gas strike was much deeper than expected, but it was uncharacteristically large enough to supply all of the church buildings with heating fuel as well as fifty families nearby. Coincidently, the natural gas pocket was found on August 22, 1891, The Feast of the Immaculate Heart of Mary, and still provides natural gas to the complex today.

When Father Nelson Baker died at the age of 95 on July 29, 1936, he left behind a legacy that would include an orphanage, trade school, general surgical hospital, maternity hospital, and a grand basilica that replaced the humble St. Patrick's Church. He was buried in nearby Holy Cross Cemetery next to his beloved parents. The diocese, afraid that Baker's grave may be disturbed because of his reputation as miracle worker had a thick layer of concrete poured on top of his vault. (Today, anyone visiting the site can see that dirt is still being taken away by believers to be used in healing and prayer.) After several tries for recognition by the Dioceses of Buffalo, the Vatican declared Baker a "Servant of God" in 1987, bringing him a step closer to sainthood.

He was said to have possessed the gift of bi-location enabling him to be in two places at the same time. Often those who were ill would be healed by either asking Father Baker to pray for them or having him merely touch them. After his passing, several miraculous healings took place by praying to the priest himself or having items that once belonged to him called "sacred relics" touched to critically ill patients.

Father Nelson Baker it seems still walks his beloved complex. Sightings of Baker have been observed in the Our Lady of Victory Hospital, the basement of the basilica near the gift shop, and his reflected image was witnessed in a mirror that is now located in a re-creation of his room in the small museum.

The most impressive of the many supernatural occurrences attributed to Baker happened when his remains were exhumed in March of 1999. Once the Vatican decided to place Baker on the fast track for sainthood, his remains were moved to a sarcophagus inside of Our Lady of Victory Basilica enabling more pilgrims access to his tomb for veneration. It was discovered that during the embalming process, three vials of blood removed from his corpse had not been disposed of and were placed on top of his casket in a leather pouch. After the

The former grave of Father Baker.

exhumation was completed, the blood was astonishingly still in a liquid state. After testing the blood, it was found that the red cells, even after sixty-three years, were not "broken down" and had "active hepatic enzymes." As the blood should have begun to coagulate immediately after Baker died, funeral directors and doctors were interviewed and all were at a loss as to why this had happened.

In life, Father Nelson Baker was considered a "living saint" because of his many charitable works. His accomplishments are nothing short of spectacular given the time in which he lived. The life of Father Baker also does one more thing. It provides the modern paranormal investigator a link between the activities witnessed during investigations and the belief in miracles. Many now believe that they are both caused by the same metaphysical process.

A close up of the former grave of Father Baker where dirt has been taken away by devoted followers.

"The Chapel"
Our Lady Help of Christians

A solemn promise made is one that should be kept. In the case of Joseph Batt, such a promise may have saved his life. Traveling from the Alsace-Lorraine region of eastern France, the Batt family decided to seek their fortune by emigrating to the United States. On November 11th, 1836, they boarded the ship *Mary Ann,* contemplating a new and bright future. However, this dream would hit a major stumbling block. Rough seas on the 29th battered the wooden vessel which was heavily damaged while riding out hurricane winds. With its sails and wooden masts shattered, the survival of the family looked dim. An extremely pious man, Joseph prayed to the Virgin Mary to intervene and save them from a watery grave. He also made a promise that if they all made it to American safely, he would build a chapel to honor her. Joseph Batt's prayer was answered as the storm subsided and the crippled *Mary Ann* limped into an Irish port for repairs. Once seaworthy again, she set sail, and after a journey of eighty-four days, reached an American port on February 2nd, 1837, coincidently The Feast of the Purification of Mary.

After establishing himself and becoming moderately successful, Joseph made good on his pledge. Bishop Timon granted him permission for the structure, and construction began in 1853 on a chapel that would see several additions over the following years, which included a bell and tower. A painting was commissioned to be hung near the alter depicting the Madonna and Child over a rendition of the ship *Mary Ann* sailing in rough seas.

The significance of this chapel cannot be measured by just its legacy to the Western New York area. It also has a long record of healings that have been attributed to it. It became a center for those who desperately needed to invoke the favors of the Blessed Mother. It must be remembered that during this time period, medical techniques relied mostly upon the "heroic theory" which stated that in order to get well, you must rid the body of diseased fluids, so healthy ones could be produced. Bleeding was quite common, as well as medicines made from mercury and other poisonous substances administered that would leave the patients with bleeding gums, loose teeth, and weak almost to the point of death. Faith would offer another alternative way of curing the afflicted.

In an era where faith healing was still a common practice, those who visited the Chapel seemed to have borne this out by receiving miraculous cures. Records show that in 1859, a 10-year-old boy was cured of a problem with his arteries after prayers were said. In 1860, a 3-year-old boy was cured of a rupture after two physicians were at

"The Chapel."

a loss as to what to do for a patient so young. During the Civil War we know of two wounds, caused by gunshots that were healed and the afflicted limbs becoming useful again. In 1865, a child fell under a moving wagon which crushed his arm. When the doctors examined the boy, they recommended that the shattered limb be immediately amputated. However, Mr. Batt refused their diagnosis and prayed for the boy's health to the Blessed Virgin. In a short time, the child's arm was miraculously healed. With horrific stories of the Plague still in their minds, German Catholics began to make pilgrimages to the chapel during the great Buffalo Cholera Epidemics of 1854 for deliverance from this malady. It seems that this is believed to have saved countless from the dreaded disease. Reminders of those early days still fill the back of the little church. Votive offerings hang from the walls as well as locked behind display cabinets. They are representations of human appendages, ears, noses, eyes, and even babies which needed to be healed, as well as braces and crutches that once served to support crippled limbs. As we gaze upon these relics, we are reminded of a time when healing was not confined solely to the realm of science.

When we think of the Chapel that Joseph Batt built, which is located on Union Road in Cheektowaga, New York, we can think of a time when religion played a central role in the lives of the common man. It was a time not just of toil, but also one of miracles. The Our Lady Help of Christians Chapel today serves as a reminder that with faith all things are possible.

A Place Where the Dead Speak

The First Spiritualist Temple of East Aurora

Tucked quietly away on Temple Street is the gray block First Spiritualist Temple of East Aurora. This unassuming building houses one of oldest continuing Modern Spiritualist congregations in New York State. Built in 1911 as a place to practice the religion of Modern Spiritualism, it has become a Mecca for those who wish to speak to their dearly departed loved ones or seek spiritual enlightenment.

The religion of Modern Spiritualism began on March 31, 1848, when Maggie and Katie Fox, mere children, first communicated with the spirit of a peddler who had been murdered in their rented cottage near Hydesville, New York. After having experienced frightening phenomena in the forms of loud "raps," Katie asked the spirit, "Mr. Splitfoot, do as I do," whereby she clapped her hands four times. Four raps answered her request. The children's mother, Margaret Fox, next asked, "Is this a human being that answers questions so correctly?" There was no reply. She then inquired, "Is it a spirit? If it is, make two raps." Immediately, two raps were heard. From this simple form of spirit communication would spring a philosophy of life and a new religion that by the late 1800s had spread throughout the world.

What separates the religion of Spiritualism from most other faiths is that spirit guidance is conveyed directly through an individual who is known as a medium. Simply described, a medium is a person who through training or natural ability can communicate with the dead. It is believed that entities communicates to them through the process of spirit mind to human mind telepathy. This interaction has become one of the main tenants of the religion.

Services that are held in the Temple are friendly and laid back. Traditional religious songs are sung, prayers are said, the "laying on of hands" for healing is done, and spirit communication takes place. It is during this time that mediums are invited to the podium to share messages from beyond with the congregation.

During my own training as a medium, I attended and served this Temple and heard many interesting stories. Once I was told that during the 1960s, the porch light had burned out. It was not replaced until almost a decade later because there were people who were afraid of being recognized when entering the Temple for the Wednesday evening services. Also, most congregations will enter a house of worship through the front door. Here, in East Aurora, many will enter through the back door near the parking lot. It is speculation that at one time members of the Temple felt that their anonymity would be more protected by doing so.

The years that I spent attending services at the Temple were some of the happiest of my life. It was there that I witnessed many occurrences that I now seek through my ongoing paranormal research. During our "Morris Pratt Study Group" meetings, we budding mediums experimented with a traditional method of spirit communication called "Table Tipping." This is where "sitters" would place their hands on a table while focusing their energy and intent on it. Eventually vibrations could be felt emanating from the table which became so strong that the table would start to slide, spin, and even dance on one leg. The ultimate goal of table tipping is to establish communication with those who have passed beyond the veil of death. This is achieved through raps that either can sound as if they came from the table itself or while the table is moving a leg will rise and tap out answers to questions.

An interesting thing happened as we worked with the tables. After reading about the basics of our religion, we decided to ask the spirits if what we were studying was indeed the truth. Immediately, the table answered with two raps which meant *NO*. Using what I nicknamed the "Alphabet Rapping System," we next began to recite letters and write them down when the table would create a tap. These letters would spell out words and the words would slowly spell out sentences. Eventually, we were informed by the table that there were subtle differences in what

The First Spiritualist Temple Of East Aurora.

it said was fact and what our course of study did. Two weeks later a woman from our group brought in a book published in the late 1890s in which these differences were recorded. None of us had known of the existence of this book.

As students, we often meditated in the worship area of the church and while doing so we experienced several wonderful examples of spirit phenomena. When first gathering as a group, only whispers were occasionally heard. As we grew in focus, the phenomena became more impressive. Early on we heard a loud bang and found that a hymnal had levitated from its pew shelf and fell to the floor. Once the door leading to the worship area, which is equipped with spring loaded hinges, opened and shut on its own accord. Heavy footsteps walking down the carpeted center aisle were noted, and knockings that seemed to come from the four corners of the room were heard. All of this activity culminated in what Spiritualists believe is the production of a substance called ectoplasm. Ectoplasm is produced from a mixture chemicals from the human body and spirit vibrations (through the work of a "Spirit Chemist"). One evening as I sat in a pew, it seemed to begin to vibrate softly. I asked one of the Temple board members to touch the pew and she acknowledged that it was somehow in fact vibrating. As I meditated deeper, I felt a "webby" feeling gently brush over my face and hands. Calling the rest of the class over, I asked them to place their hands into what I can only call a floating mass of energy. All in the class felt something like cotton candy or spider webs. While we did not actually see anything with our eyes, each one of us experienced the phenomena through touch.

So can The First Spiritualist Temple of East Aurora be considered a haunted location? Absolutely. However, those who visit the Temple are asked to do so with respect. All should remember that this is a house of worship, a place where the dead surely speak.

Chapter 14

The Vanishing Hitchhiker of Sugar Road

Urban Legends are the things that teenage nightmares are made from. Perhaps one of the most common and enduring legends of them all is of that of the "Vanishing Hitchhiker." This story is one that has been told and retold since the dawn of the automotive age. Most of these accounts began to surface around the time of the Great Depression and have morphed with each growing generation of teens. It comes in all variations and is found virtually in every part of the United States as well as Canada. The one common thread is that the person who tells this story swears that he heard it from someone whom actually experienced it!

As we know, there are certain locations in Western New York that are perfect for legends and stories of the paranormal. Roads that are often bordered by places of burial are rich in such lore. In Cheektowaga, New York, there is such a place where teenagers have tested their courage against the unseen spirits that roam the night. One such location is a short stretch of asphalt named Sugar Road.

Connecting Pine Ridge to Eggert Roads, Sugar Road is part of what forms a large necropolis. It should also be noted that Pine Ridge Road is literally referred to as one of the creepiest byways in the Buffalo area. From Genesee Street till its end where Route 33 literally cuts a path through St. Stanislous Cemetery, it is surrounded by places of burial. Every culture and nationality is represented along this poorly lit and lonely stretch of roadway. Generations of Polish, French, German, Catholic, Protestant, and Jewish families have laid their loved one to rest along this side street. Often only the muted, red light of vigil candles lovingly placed at the graves of relations give this area its illumination.

Many years ago, there was once a caretakers home located on the corner of Pine Ridge and Sugar Road. It was a plain frame building that was demolished sometime before the 1990s and now is filled with graves. As is told by those who swear by its truth, a man driving down

Pine Ridge Road, from Walden Avenue saw a pretty young girl in an angora sweater walking during a heavy rainstorm. Being the chivalrous type, he stopped and asked if she needed a ride, to which she smiled and replied *yes*. Jumping into the car, the driver noticed that his passenger would only stare straight ahead, never making any type of eye contact. Asking where she was going she replied, "Home, just down the road a little ways."

After stopping for the light at the intersection of Genesee Road, they continued forth, past the many cemeteries to where he saw a cemetery caretaker's house. The driver asked, "Is this where you really live?" Turning when he received no reply, he saw that there was only a red rose placed on a very damp seat.

Shocked at this experience, the driver pulled to the side of the road and went up to the house and rang the bell. An elderly man answered the door and asked if the driver was lost. The driver recounted his story to which the man answered that the hitchhiker was his daughter. She had been raped and murdered some years before and he had been not the first to bring her home. Each time someone picked her up, a single rose was left on the front seat where she had once sat. Shaken at this revelation, the driver asked the name of his daughter. The man replied, "Rose."

The site of the Old Caretaker's House near Sugar Road.

Fact or fantasy, most urban legends have roots in reality. Could this have been actually based on a true story? All that is known is that on dark, raining nights, Sugar Road is one of those places best avoided except for those who wish to experience the Legend of Rose.

Chapter 15

Spooks About Town and Other Sites of Macabre Interest

The Jersey Street Engine House

Fire Engine #7, Hook and Ladder #9

Following the American Civil War, Buffalo experienced a time of prosperity and growth. As the nation's "premier inland port," it became evident that the city was beginning to outgrow its old waterfront neighborhoods. Initially, the new homes of the growing workforce were built in what is now the Allentown District. Quickly and cheaply constructed, these structures sprang up at a rapid pace. Accompanying this blue collar influx came with it an upscale class of citizens who also wished to find space to build their homes. In 1868, architect Frederick Law Olmstead and his partner Calvert Vaux were commissioned to design a park system with residential streets that linked several "urban green spaces" together. With this design in place many influential citizens began constructing their mansions on nearby Symphony Circle in 1874.

With the spike in new housing, there arose a need for more fire protection. In an age where furnaces were still fired by coal and indoor lighting was provided by oil lamps and gas outlets, fire posed a serious threat. Realizing that these new neighborhoods would need protection, Department Superintendent Joseph R. Williams suggested that a new firehouse be built. After deliberations, it was decided that the structure should be constructed on the corner of Jersey and Plymouth Streets. However, it was rumored that the location was selected because William G. Fargo, the ex mayor and a powerful businessman, wanted a firehouse close to his mansion. Property nearby Fargo's estate was purchased for $3,000 from the Jersey Street Methodist Episcopal Church whose original house of worship located there had ironically burned several years earlier.

The building was designed by the architectural firm of Porter and Watkins at a cost of $10,020. It is considered a fine example of the

The Old Firehouse.

Second Empire style, built with red brick and having arched windows with ornamental trims, dormers, a highly pitched mansard slate roof, high ceilings covered with tin sheeting, slab marble bathroom stall dividers, hot and cold running water, and most importantly, a system whereby steam was channeled from the building's furnace to keep the fire engine "stoked" at all times. It also boasted, along with the necessary fire fighting equipment, four horses, a sleigh, a wagon, seven walnut bedsteads, fine tables, seven armchairs, carpets, seventeen spittoons, as well as five chandeliers. The Firehouse was opened on December 14th, 1875, and it was considered a marvel of modern technology. Later, in 1896, an addition designed by the firm of Eckel & Ackerman was added.

On January 8th, 1917, the unthinkable happened. A fire within the station ignited and quickly roared out of control gutting the interior of the building. The new gasoline-powered American LaFrance pumper truck, one of the first in the region that had been stationed there, fell through the burnt wooden floor and into the basement. Several firefighters escaped the blaze by crawling through second-story windows. Although there were no fatalities, many of the firefighters did suffer burns and most probably smoke inhalation.

This grand relic of a more opulent time was deactivated in 1997 when a new station was built nearby. The building was designated as a historic landmark in 1998 and has been sold to a private owner. While conducting renovations, workmen have reported hearing strange noises, whispers, and footsteps, as well as a feeling that they were being watched.

In February 2008, I joined Darren and Jenn Pogue in an investigation of the former firehouse. Upon conducting the initial walk through, it was discovered that there were several areas of high EMF that emanated from a transformer and wiring sources. This could account for the feelings of being watched. A complete investigation was conducted, however, no solid evidence was captured that evening. This being the case team members decided to try to detect the presence of energy by using dowsing rods. Immediately after asking the rods to locate the source of the energy, the rods reacted strongly near the second-floor window where the figure of a man has been reported. Communication with spirit entities associated with the location was attempted with only limited success. From the dowsing experiments conducted, it was concluded that while there may have been psychokinetic energy present during that particular investigation, there was no communication to indicate that there was an intelligence behind the reported phenomena. However, it should be noted that the team investigated the building for only a five-hour period. While we did discover pockets of energy, we cannot rule out that there is an absence of spirit activity at other times.

Asbestos dust orbs.

Today, we are thankful that this watchful brick matron from another age has been saved from the wrecking ball. Within its walls may lie many secrets that yet wait to be discovered. Ask any seasoned paranormal investigator and they will tell you that sometimes one investigation is simply not enough.

The Michael J. Dillon Federal Courthouse

The importance of the City of Buffalo to the region can never be disputed. In the early twentieth century, it was the location of the region's Federal governmental agencies as well as its court system. These administrative offices were scattered throughout the city so it became necessary for a facility to be built in order to house them all at one location. Unfortunately, a Great Depression had swept through the United States causing vast unemployment and poverty. In an effort to get people back to work, The Emergency Relief and Construction Act was passed by Congress in 1932, making it possible to find the necessary funding for this project and get the local economy going again.

This courthouse is located at 64 Court Street and was designed by Lawrence Blay, Duane Lyman and E.B. Green and Son. Its unique architecture, dictated by the shape of the site, resulted in a seven-story building that is pentagonal shaped. Most importantly, the building incorporates many examples of Art Deco Geometric Designs which is considered a form of "sacred architecture" that seems to feed energy into paranormally active locations.

Retired Federal Agent Greg Hoffman who worked in the building for many years can tell many unsettling stories about his time spent there. Often on the evening shift, after the offices had closed, he heard footsteps crossing the empty lobby, many times sounding as if whoever it was wore squeaky, wet galoshes. Other times, a radio located on his desk would turn on by itself. Of interest are the larger scale electrical anomalies that would happen. Elevators would operate by themselves as well as having their emergency alarms go off when no one was around. Probably most unnerving were the sounds of moaning that was occasionally encountered.

What could be the cause of these nocturnal events? Greg tells of a security guard who may have committed suicide just before he started. Could he still be the source for these supernatural activities? Is he just walking his old beat or could it just be the result of mindless energy that has built up because of the architecture of the location? Regardless of its source, this is part of Buffalo's proud and quite mysterious heritage.

Hamlin House

The former residence of Cicero J. Hamlin, a wealthy sugar investor, was built in the late 1800s of red brick in the Italian Villa-style that was popular in rural northern Italy. Its location on Franklin Street assured a quiet suburban lifestyle yet was close enough to Buffalo's Commerce district for an easy commute. During this time period, Franklin Street had the distinction of being a place where many in the medical profession chose to live and work thus earning the nickname of "Pill Alley."

Over the years, the Hamlin House has had several reoccurring examples of paranormal phenomena. Footsteps are often heard along the second floor hallway that leads to a balcony which overlooks the banquet hall. It is whispered that rhythmic tapping takes place when slower music is played accompanied by the smell of a rich cigar. Also, the sounds of chairs being moved and the clank of moving dishes can be heard when the building is closed to the public. Many seem to feel that this phenomena is attributed to the ghost of Circero Hamlin who may still walk the floors of his former home.

The Hamlin House.

Today this building is home to the American Legion Post 665 and the Hamlin House Restaurant and Banquet Hall.

The Market Arcade

Buffalo's Original Haunted Shopping Mall

When the Market Arcade was opened by G.B. Marshal, it was a awe-inspiring shopping experience. Designed in 1892 by E.B. Green, it was based on the European-style markets that offered space for offices and shops along a street enclosed by a sort of archway. Located at 639 Main Street, it provided shoppers with a "civilized" three-story urban setting where patrons could browse the wares of several different stores regardless of weather conditions. The large scale use of plate glass store fronts as well as frosted-glass skylights, and elaborate iron work gives the interior a rich and comforting feel. Also, the structure itself incorporates many elements of "sacred geometry," such as Corinthian Columns, Carved Keystones, and Romanesque Arches which are common in buildings of that era. It has been found that the use of "sacred geometry" does have an effect on paranormal activity, sometimes increasing the strength of the phenomena.

As the downtown business district began to lose its shoppers to the sprawling plazas of the suburbs in the 1960s, the Market Arcade suffered neglect and became vacant for a number of years. Recently under new ownership and management, it has begun to enjoy a revival and is now one of the city's cultural centers.

There are various stories of paranormal activity occurring throughout the building. It has been reported that a jeweler was murdered on the second floor and sounds of crashing objects are now heard in the retail space below it. People have seen shadow beings who seemingly disappear when spotted, as well as after hours heavy footsteps and furniture being moved about are often heard. Perhaps the activity has been caused by a few ghostly shoppers from the late nineteenth century taking a stroll though a location that was highly impressive and enjoyable to them. It is more likely that it is the combination of the structures attributes as well as its long history that may lend itself to a residual haunting. In any event, the Market Arcade is must "stop and visit" location along haunted Main Street in the old Nickel City.

The Paranormal ABCs
Haunted Elementary Schools

Often it is taken for granted that children seem to possess a strong psychic sense. Perhaps this is due to them not being told that this ability is either wrong or something to fear. When researching children and their effect upon physical phenomenon, it is often discovered that they can achieve a variety of activities that most adults would find unnerving. Could it be that a child's boundless energy is really psychokinetic in nature? If this be the case, then it is reasonable to assume that a child could leave behind a sort of "energy imprint" at a location where they once played or attended school?

For most people, an Elementary School is a non threatening place. Surrounded by examples of artwork made from macaroni and the familiar smell of cafeteria food, it produces a feeling of security that we remember from a far simpler time. However, this does not grant immunity to such a building from spectral visitors. Here are two such places that may prove that the security we may feel, might just be deceiving.

Woodrow Wilson Elementary School

Woodrow Wilson Elementary School is a red brick, three-story structure built in 1931 which serves the Cheektowaga-Sloan Union Free School District. Located on the corner of Halstead Street and Reiman Avenue in the Village of Sloan, New York, it has been an active center for early learning for many years. In 1993, a woman was hired to fill a temporary position with its cleaning staff. One evening, after completing her duties on the third floor, she witnessed the apparition of a woman wearing a long flowing evening dress that seemed to float from classroom to classroom. After this frightening personal experience, she decided to contact others who had also held the same position previous to her being hired. Each validated her experience by affirming that they too had also seen this same apparition.

To this day, no one knows who this lady is or why she walks the halls of Woodrow Wilson School. What they *do* know is that this mysterious lady never appears in any way that would frighten young children. So for now this non threatening spirit shall be one of the nameless many who walk lightly upon this earthly plane.

Woodrow Wilson Elementary School.

The Alexander Street Elementary School

At the former Alexander Street Elementary School, a classic haunting has been taking place for several years. Closed during a district restructuring program, the school was taken over and is now used as a Municipal Building for the Township of Cheektowaga. In order for this former primary school to be readied for its new public life, much remodeling was needed. It is common knowledge among paranormal investigators that by altering an existing structure, psychokinetic energies can be disturbed causing a host of interesting phenomenon.

Most recently, an evening maintenance worker refused to go there and requested a transfer to a different facility. His reason was that he

The former Alexander Street Elementary School building.

became terrified of the unexplained noises that he experienced on a regular basis. The sounds of footsteps, doors closing, rappings, and whispers were often heard. After a short time, these sounds became enough to convince him that he did not wish to stay there after dark.

So what were the sources of these frightening sounds? Could it have been a disturbance of long dormant energies that fed this seemingly residual haunting? Or could it have been the workings of one person's imagination after being locked in a large building after dark. We may never know for sure, however, for one worker, he plainly did not wish to stay and find out.

Chapter 16

Those Who Spoke to the Dead

The Reverend Jack Kelly

Ordained Minister, Healer, Medium, Missionary: These are impressive credentials for any Spiritualist worker. However, when researching the life of the Reverend John T. Kelly, words seem to become inadequate. Simply known as "Jack" Kelly to his Buffalo and Lily Dale, New York congregations, this twentieth century personage looms larger than life.

Jack was born on August 3, 1899 in Marthytown, Wales. It has been reported that the "gift" was naturally occurring from childhood and that his father was also a sensitive. Around the age of five or six years old Jack was walking home from school. As he was crossing a pasture he had a vision of a fire wagon drawn by four or five horses racing across the sky. Young Jack went home and told his mother what he had seen. The following day the barn on a neighboring farm burned to the ground.

Like many of his other teenaged countrymen, he was employed as a coal miner until the outbreak of the First World War. Serving in the Royal Field Artillery, Jack was wounded three times. His stepson, Robert Zagora, has told me that "his teacher" used to tell him who was going survive (the war) and who would not. "The teacher would say this guy was going to make it and that guy wouldn't. A day or two later…they would be gone." The rest of his unit was afraid to ask him who might be next as his predictions always seemed to come true. Jack once told a guy who was driving an ammunition wagon that he was going to make it. He was injured but survived the War. Such were his wartime experiences. After the signing of the Treaty of Versailles, Jack was discharged from the British Army on January 23, 1919.

Kelly had become an ardent Spiritualist and medium before immigrating to the United States, eventually settling in Buffalo, New York. He founded the Church of Life and became a distinguished

Platform Worker in the Spiritualist Camp located at Lily Dale. Along with administering to the spiritual needs of his local community, Jack traveled internationally and was even once issued a challenge by the London Society of Magicians. The magicians found it impossible to duplicate Jack's psychic demonstrations.

The Reverend Kelly had many abilities for which he was well known, but he excelled at "Billet Reading." He would issue a challenge for someone to come up and tightly tie a cloth over his eyes to the point of not even being able to blink. People attending this type of demonstration were asked to write on a piece of paper (referred to as a billet) a question which was placed in a container. Jack would reach in take a billet and answer it correctly. After this was done, he would toss the paper into a trash can while still blindfolded. There is a story that a boy named Bryon Candi once moved the basket with his foot attempting to be funny. Without looking Jack said "Bryon, you put that back where it belongs."

Those who still speak of the Rev. Kelly discuss the merits of his gift of healing. In fact, the Healing Temple located in Lily Dale was built for his ministry and it was said that he himself contributed to the building costs. Jack is especially remembered for a healing that was reported in *The Dunkirk Observer* on August 3, 1952. Mrs. Donna Ball of Pittsford, New York, had been badly injured in an automobile accident which left her blind in both eyes along with a paralyzed right hand. Mrs. Ball attended a healing service in the Lily Dale auditorium. Reverend Kelly performed a healing by "laying on the hands" which was witnessed by approximately forty people. As she was leaving the building, her eyesight returned as well as regaining some strength in her hand.

Jack had many admirers from all walks of life. The famous film actress, Mae West, was counted among them. The story goes that he had been working at the National Spiritualist Association Convention held in Los Angeles in 1941. A local newspaper had published a short article about the Spiritualist's meeting. Mae must have read it, and as she was interested in the metaphysical world, became intrigued. She could not go herself because people might take advantage of her because of her notoriety. Mae said to her business manager, "You go down and see if you can find anybody worth while. You should take somebody with you." At the time, she had a stage show consisting of professional wrestlers billed as "Mae West and the Twelve Strongest Men in the World." So the manager took a fellow by the name of Jim Stanley. They attended services and filled out a billet. Jim Stanley's billet was picked and Jack said to him, "Your name is really [the original name is not known at this time] and he spelled it out using eleven letters. That's your family name!" The two men looked at each other. Finally Mae's manager asked, "Is that your name? It's a Polish name! I always thought you were a Latin because you are so dark. I thought you were either Spanish or Italian or something." He said, "No I'm Polish." Kelly then continued on by saying that his father (who was in spirit) said that his death was not a natural one. He was hit over the head during the war. Jim Stanley said, "Yes, we found his body during the war. We thought that it was an accident." Mae West was so impressed with Jack Kelly's abilities that he was often a guest at her beach house in Santa Monica, California, where he would do readings and demonstrations for many of her celebrity friends.

Reverend Kelly also possessed the ability to produce a spirit voice through his solar plexus. During a recent interview, Mr. Zagora informed me that Jack's "teacher" would carry on the dialog with spirit people, and it was the voice of spirit talking back and forth. In fact, sometimes he would call you up and directly talk to spirit. There was (once) a woman who asked for a message from her little girl (who had passed). He picked the message up from the teacher while in trance and he said that:

> "You asked about your daughter. Come on up here to the platform. Your little darling is right here." The woman came up and started balling her eyes out. "I'll step aside and let her talk to you." The voice was saying, 'Please don't cry mother. I'm Okay. There are a lot of little children around here. I'm doing alright. Please I don't want you to be so sad.' The more the she talked about it the more the mother cried. She was weeping so loud that finally her husband ran up to her and grabbed her and took her back to her seat and she was still crying. It's sort of touching that the girl was trying to reassure her mother up at the platform saying that she is alright. I don't know how old she was but it sounded like a young voice.

Reverend Kelly also made several predictions. In one he stated that there will be a warming trend in the weather, and that farmers will be growing peanuts in the state of Maine. This prediction was made approximately fifty years ago when the concern of global warming was fodder for a science fiction writer's imagination.

It seems that healings were not always for the people who attended his services. Robert Zagora once again relates the following story.

> He (Jack) fell off the chair while watching TV after he taught a class. He was sitting there and we heard a loud crash and we ran into the room and saw that he had fallen, probably on his side and my mother sort of tipped him back. She said, "I have to open his shirt because 'they' (his spirit guides) are trying to tell me something," so she put her ear to his solar plexus and a voice said that he had a stroke. She (was told to) loosen his tie and put him on the couch. After a few minutes his "teacher" came in and started working on

him. And as he was working on him, he (Jack's guide, White Hawk) started talking to another voice (Dr. Barrington, also a guide). One (spirit guide) was talking through his solar plexus and one was talking through his mouth. As they were working on him, they held a conversation. The physician was saying where he needed the most work and using sort of medical terms that I didn't understand. They kept working on him and kept cracking his neck and loosening him up for about fifteen minutes. All the time they worked on him they carried on a conversation, these two spirit entities. They were telling each other what to do. They worked on him in the physical so (they) had to use a physical voice to communicate with one another. It took about fifteen minutes; then it was stopped. My mother went over to him and they said, "He'll be alright; he's had a stroke but we caught it in time. Don't say anything to him about what happened because he's only going to worry about it. (Jack's teachers then said) Put him back in his chair. Before you leave the room put the TV back on." That's what we did. After a while (he came out), and he said that he had a terrific headache and a stiff neck but he didn't know what really happened to him.

After Jack retired, he moved to Estaboga, Alabama, with his third wife. In his later years, Jack Kelly developed what is believed to have been lung cancer. His failing health had been caused by his early exposure to coal dust and his habit of smoking two packs of cigarettes a day. The Reverend Jack Kelly passed into spirit on November 18, 1964. However, physical death was not the end of his story. Mae West who had first met Jack so many years previously received a visitation from the famous late medium. She recalled that,

> It was eight o'clock in the evening… First, I heard this voice, a deep voice, and I knew it wasn't the television. I couldn't make out what it said, but I turned and saw feet. You see as I turned I looked at the floor and I saw a man's shoes and his legs or rather his trousers. Then I looked up and there was Jack Kelly sitting on the couch next to me, just as real and solid as he had ever been, only looking much younger than when he died 10 or 12 years ago. There wasn't a line in his face and he was more than 60 when he passed on… Kelly (then) dissolved right down through the couch – not too fast, but not slow either. It was a tremendous thing – the way he dissolved right before my eyes…and was gone.

It was said that Jack was dressed in a formal tuxedo when he appeared to Mae. Mae West, at the time of her death, had been writing and researching a book entitled *The Amazing Mr. Kelly*, however, the manuscript has never been found.

Reverend Jack Kelly was an incredibly talented medium who has become one of the notables in the history of American Spiritualism. He touched the lives of many and we who follow in his footsteps owe him a debt of gratitude for the inspiration that his legacy has given us.

Flo Cottrell and The Fox Cottage

Born in 1884, Flo Cottrell was born in Holland, New York in 1884. As with most mediums of her era, she realized that she possessed the ability to channel spirit communication to the world at a very young age. During the late 1800s the religion of Spiritualism was one of the fastest growing religions in the United States. Young Flo was exposed to it through her Aunt and Uncle who would often conduct "table tipping" séances in her home. She recalled that "the table would levitate easily if I had my fingers on it. I was just a young girl then. Soon we would get faint raps on the middle of the table."

Miss Cottrell eventually joined the religion and became highly regarded within the Lily Dale Spiritualist Community and at the Spiritualist churches in nearby Buffalo. Having achieved such status, Flo was asked to frequently speak at many Spiritualist services as well as being the keynote speaker at the opening of the First Spiritualist Temple in East Aurora, New York in 1911. There she was able to demonstrate the ability to communicate to Spirits through the sounds of discarnate knockings.

Of the many things that Flo Cottrell is fondly remembered, it was she who was the medium who worked in the original Fox Cottage considered the birthplace of the Spiritualist Movement. Originally built in Hydesville, New York, it was moved to Lily Dale in 1915. The cottage itself was a humble wood-framed dwelling built by Dr. Henry Hyde in 1815. It is known that from 1842 to 1843, the house was rented by the Bell family. It was during this time that the ill-fated peddler, Charles Rosna, called upon them and disappeared. The Bell's housekeeper, Lucretia Pulver, had been promptly dismissed from service when Rosna arrived yet was mysteriously rehired shortly afterwards. Mrs. Bell gave Lucretia several items and trinkets that she claimed to have purchased from the peddler. It was shortly thereafter that raps were heard at the foot of Lucretius's bed. The Bells explained that there were rats in the walls making noise. However, the raps began in earnest to the point it began disturbing Mr. and Mrs. Bell. Also in the course of her duties, Lucretia went into the cellar and slipped into a large sink hole that had never previously been noticed. There was a lot of loose dirt on the earthen floor and again rats were blamed. Shortly thereafter, Mr. Bell had more dirt brought into the cellar and stones were then stored there (for the purpose of supposedly building a fence). As the rappings continued, Lucretia left her employment. Mrs.

Bell's health took a turn for the worse and the family left the cottage. (Later neighbors wrote depositions exonerating the Bells of any wrong doings and bore witness to their good character, but the stain to their reputation remained.)

The next tenants from 1843 to 1846 were the Weeks Family. An entire year had passed peacefully until raps were once again heard. One of the Weeks daughters received the cold touch of a hand and the housekeeper saw the specter of a "young, sandy-haired man [dressed] in grey trousers and a black jacket." Phenomena continued, however, it was forbidden to be spoken about in the house. The Weeks family moved and the cottage remained vacant until December of 1847.

It was during that year the Fox family found itself seeking a new start. John Fox suffered from alcoholism and he and his wife, Margaret, had separated. Upon embracing sobriety, John reunited with his family. The couple had older children dating from the time previous to their breakup and now had two more, Margaretta (born 1834) and Catherine (born 1836). Searching for a rural area, they moved temporarily into a home that adjoined an uncle's property. The family took possession of the Hydesville cottage on December 11, 1847. It would be here that John intended to live while he built his own house as well as operating a "smithy" business.

Throughout their stay, mysterious rappings and other phenomena occurred. Finally, on March 31, 1848, the age of modern spirit communication was born. Mrs. Fox gives the following narrative:

> The children in the other room heard the rapping and tried to make similar sounds by snapping their fingers. My youngest child (Cathie/Katie) said, "Mr. Splitfoot, do as I do," clapping her hands. The sound imitated her with the same number of raps. The children, as well as Mrs. Fox, tested this phenomena by asking the entity to rap out the correct ages of the children, which it did. The question of whether it was a spirit gained two raps to which the Fox family had assigned a "yes" answer. They asked if the spirit had been injured in the house and through the use of the verbal recitation of the alphabet (the spirit would rap when it came to a letter that it needed to spell out a word) they established the story of the murdered peddler.

When word got out, the cottage was deluged by religious, curious, and thrill-seeking citizens. The family was forced to seek refuge in older son David Fox's home a few miles away. Even representatives of the Shaker religion came to Hydesville to verify the communication as well as the fulfillment of Mother Lee's Prophesy of 1830. In this prophesy, it was stated that the Shakers were told that their "gifts" would be "withdrawn and poured out upon all of the people of the world – with a promised new era to be inaugurated by extraordinary discoveries of material and spiritual wealth." (Gold was discovered in California in1849 and the "Hydesville rappings" began in 1848). The "voice" told the Shakers that when the power returned, spirits would pervade the world and enter palace as well as cottage. With all of this fan fair and excitement, the religion of Modern Spiritualism became one of the fastest growing religions in the United States.

As time passed, the cellar floor was dug up revealing broken crockery, traces of charcoal, quicklime, hair and bone. The bones were examined and declared that of a human skull. Years later in 1904, school children playing in the cellar of the cottage found more bones when a wall collapsed. The owner, Mr. William Hyde, investigated these claims and found an almost complete skeleton.

Over the years, the cottage eventually fell into disrepair. Local children (as well as adults) called it "the spook house." To save it from the ongoing vandalism, the cottage was purchased by B.F. Bartlett in 1915, dismantled and moved to the Spiritualist Camp located in Lily Dale, New York, the following year. There it would inspire and educate generations of visitors and Spiritualists alike.

The high point of the religious work done through the Fox Cottage was a demonstration of the raps heard by the Fox family. It was Flo Cottrell who conducted these demonstrations of spirit communication. She would place her hand upon a beam in the reconstructed cellar (referred to as "the rapping beam") and produce spirit communication. This she did between the hours of "10:00 to 12:00 and 4:00 to 6:00" (She stated that her "spirit teacher" had instructed her on what hours to keep the cottage open and conduct demonstrations. Admission, by the way, to the cottage was twenty-five cents). Flo Cottrell continued these demonstrations until the destruction of the cottage.

According to newspaper reports in the early hours of September 21, 1955, a fire raged through the cottage. It was noticed by Mrs. William Truesdale, a neighbor at 3:30am, and despite all efforts, very little could be saved. The cause was listed as "spontaneous combustion," however to this day, many in "the Dale" still feel that it may have been arson. It was reported that the windows had been boarded up and the building closed since Labor Day of that year.

The woman who followed the path of the Fox Sisters and described as someone who was "sweet and shy" passed from this world on October 3rd, 1962. Her many friends and family gathered at the Spiritualist Temple in East Aurora, New York, where many years before she had been its first speaker. Her earthly remains were laid to rest in the Protection Rural Cemetery in her native Holland, New York. Her life a testament to the belief that communication with the dead is a fact proven through mediumship.

Bibliography

Anderson Floyd. Apostle of Charity. Our Lady of Victory Homes of Charity. 2002.

Atwell, Glenn. Batt, Ronald. *The Chapel.* The Holling Press, Inc., Buffalo, NY, 1979.

Associated Press. "National Recognition Sought for Cemetery from War of 1812." May 8, 2002.

Barber, Steve. "Washington Street Closed Over Concerns Of Collapse." WKBW.Com. September 2, 2008.

Barnes, Sandra. Personal Interview. 2010.

Bean, Bill. *Delivered.* Self Published, 2010.

Berton, Pierrre. "Flames Across the Border." *Atlantic Monthly Press*, 1981.

Blia, Adam. Personal Interview. 2010.

Boyd, Doug. *Mad Bear*. Touchtone Books, New York, NY, 1994.

Brittle, Gerald. *The Demonologist.* iUniverse, Lincoln, NE, 1980.

Brunvand, Jan Harold. *The Vanishing Hitchhiker, American Urban Legends & Their Meanings*, W.N. Norton & Co., Inc., Toronto, Ontario, 1981

Brown, Christopher N. "Historic Plymouth Avenue in the Kleinhans District." www.buffaloah.com, 2008.

Brown, Christopher N. "Historic Plymouth Avenue in the Kleinhans District." www.buffaloah.com, 2008.

Buckham, Tom. "1813 Citizen – Hero Finally Will Receive Recognition." *The Buffalo News*, May 22, 2008.

Buckland, Raymond. *The Spirit Book.* Visible Ink, Canton, MI, 2006.

Buffalo Federal Court House. www.buffaloah.com/a/court/64/index.html.

Bulletin of the Buffalo Society of Natural Sciences, 1908.

Burke, Tom. "Mae West in New York." *New York Times*. http//journals.aol.com/nonstop/MaeWest/entries/2005/05/02.

Byrne, Thomas. "The Sullivan – Clinton Campaign of 1779." Chemung County Historical Society, Inc., 1979.

Bipedal, Bob. "The Story of Cheektowaga's Ghost Trestle." Unknown publication.

Buffalo News. "City Honors Site May Yield More Forgotten Graves." 6/10/08.

City of Buffalo. http://www.ci.buffalo.ny.us/.

Conlin, John H. *The Historian's Notebook, Tommy Jemmy*. Western New York Heritage, Summer 2008.

Courier-Express, "Fire Levels Fox Cottage at Lily Dale." Date unavailable.

Crocitto, John. Personal Interview, 2009.

Dafoe, Stephen, Morgan. *The Scandal That Shook Freemasonry.* Cornerstone Books Publishers, New Orleans, LA, 2009.

Davis, Rodney, *Dowsing. The Aquarian Press*, Hammersmith, London, 1991.

Delaney, Barbara A. "Grave Hunting With Ground Penetrating Radar at the Historic Hull House Cemetery." gsa.confex.com/gsa/2006AM/finalprogram/abstract_113388. htm, 2006.

Densmore, Christopher. *Red Jacket, Iroquois Diplomat and Orator.* Syracuse University Press, Syracuse, NY 1999.

Dittmar, Willard B. *Tolerable Tales of the Tonawandas*, The Historical Society of the Tonawandas, Inc, 1993.

Division of Archives and History, Commemoration Committee of the Sullivan – Clinton Campaign In 1779, 1929.

The Dunkirk Observer, "Pittsford Woman gets Sight Back." *August 3, 1952,* Lily Dale Historical Society.

Dunnigan, Brian Leigh. *Forts With A Fort.* Old Fort Niagara Association, 1989.

Dunnigan, Brian Leigh & Scott, Patricia. *Old Fort Niagara in Four Centuries.* Old Fort Niagara Association, 1991.

Fate Magazine. 1963, 1977.

Finch, Roy G. *The Story of the New York States Canals*. NYS Canal Corporation, 1925.

Fredericks, Jeff. Buffalo Terminal EVP evidence.

Full Circle Studio's, The Phantom Tour, 13 Most Haunted Places in WNY, 2003.

German Catholic Orphanage, WWW.BuffaloResearch.com.

Hastreiter, Linda. Interview, *The Black Cat Lounge* Radio Hour.

Hill, Dave. "Author Explains Why The Tonawanda's Are So Spooky." *Tonawanda News*, 10/3/08.

Holtz, Mary F. and Nowicki, Lee. *The Bennet Family Cemetery*, 2000.

Kavanagh, Kevin. "History of Women in Forest Lawn Cemetery, Sarah Lovejoy." www.buffaloah.com/a/forestL/lovejoy/index.html, 2000.

Kellerman, Gladys. President of The First Spiritualist Temple of East Aurora, Personal Conversations and Sermons, 1999.

Knoerl, T. Kurt. USS *The Sullivans* DD537, The Buffalo & Erie Co., Naval Park.

Koerner, John. *The Mysteries of Father Baker,* Western New York Wares, Inc., Buffalo, NY, 2005.

Koerner, John. *The Father Baker Codex*, Western New York Wares, Inc., Buffalo, NY, 2009.

Kowsky, Francis R. "History of Market Arcade." www.buffaloah.com/a/main/617/hp.html, 2002.

Kupczyk, Robert E. "Phantoms of the Opera House." Amherst Bee, October 26, 2005.

Kwitchoff, Artie. Correspondence, Town Ballroom.

Lancaster Opera House. www.lancopera.org.

Lankes, Frank J. *The Ebenezer Community of True Inspiration*. Liesling Printing Company, West Seneca, NY, 1949.

Lankes, Frank J. *An Old Ebenezer Graveyard Mystery*. West Seneca Historical Society Pamphlet, 1965.

Lankes, Frank J. *Reservation Supplement*. West Seneca Historical Society, 1966.

Lankes, Frank J. "The Seneca's On Buffalo Creek Reservation." West Seneca, NY, 1964.

Leary, Thomas E. & Sholes, Elizabeth C. *Buffalo's Waterfront*. Arcadia Publishing, Charleston, SC, 1997.

Licata, Elizabeth, "Fear and Loathing and Sex and Death, Buffalo Style." Buffalo Spree, December, 2008.

Lily Dale Historical Museum. Rev J. T. Kelly File.

Lockhart, Rob. Correspondence.

Long, Archbishop James. *Through the Eyes of an Exorcist.* Self Published 2007.

Martin, Malichi. *Hostage To The Devil.* HarperSanFransico Edition, San Fransico, CA, 1992.

Mendola, Nicholas. "One Reporter, One Haunted Castle, One Night." *Niagara Gazette*, 10/31/05.

Morris Pratt Institute. *Educational Course on Modern Spiritualism.* Morris Pratt Institute Association, 1999.

National Spiritualist Association of Churches. www.nsac.org.

Natti, Todd. "An Orphan Of History." *Artvoice*, 10/26/06.

North Tonawanda Historical Society, "Black Hannah." www.northtonawanda.org/images/cemetery/cemetery_legend.htm.

North Tonawanda Historical Society. "Sweeney Cemetery."

http://www.northtonawanda.org/images/cemetery/cemetery_history.htm.

Percy, John W. Tonawanda, *The Way It Was*, Partner's Press, Inc., Tonawanda, NY, 1979.

Peters, Arlan. Shea's Performing Arts Center, Official Page, www.Buffaloah.com, January 2006.

Peters, Arlan. Shea's Buffalo Theatre/Shea's Performing Arts Center, Timeline, www.Buffaloah.com, 2006.

Priger, Bill. "Railroad Slang." http://www.vnerr.com/news/slang.htm.

Pinsky, Mark A. *The EMF Book*, Warner Books, New York, NY, 1995.

Porter, Peter. Niagara Falls, 1896. www.archive.org/details/cu31924028824831, 1896.

Pouchot, Pierre. *Memoirs of the Late War in North America Between France and England. T*ranslated by Michael Cady, Old Fort Niagara Association, 1994.

Psychic Observer. "Flo Cottrell Holds Unique Place Among Modern Mediums." Undated.

Rapp, Marvin A. *Canal Water and Whiskey.* The Heritage Press, Buffalo, NY, 1992.

Shaw, Timothy. Investigative Case Logs. 1995 through 2009.

Sieben, Bob. "The Riviera Theatre and Its Mighty Wurlitzer Pipe Organ." http://www.rivieratheater.org/. Accessed 2009.

Stone, William L. *The Life and Times of Red Jacket or Sa – Go – Ye – Wat – Ha*, Wiley and Putnum, www.archive.org/details/timesofredjacket00stonrich, 1841.

Sunseri, Alvin and Lyftogt, Kenneth. *The Sullivan Family of Waterloo. 1988*. Friends of the Waterloo Public Library. Waterloo, IA.

Smith, H. Perry. *History of Buffalo and Erie. County.* www.buffaloah.com/a/forestL/pratt_s/source/1.html, 1884.

Snow, Dean R. *The Iroquois.* Blackwell Publishers. Cambridge, MA,1994.

Swinnich, James W. *USS* Croaker *SS-246*, The Buffalo & Erie Co. Naval & Military Park. 2009.

The Shadowlands: "Ghosts and Hauntings." www.Shadowlands.net. Accessed 2009.

War of 1812 quotes, www.shmoop.com.

Webster, Richard. *Dowsing for Beginners*, Llewellyn Publications, St. Paul, MN, 1996.

West Seneca Historical Society, *Kau-qua-tau, Indian Woman Accused of Sorcery*, Self Published Pamphlet. West Seneca, NY.

Whipking, Jenna. Personal Interview, 2009.

White, Glenn. Personal Interview, 2009.

Winfield, Mason. *Haunted Places of Western New York*, Western New York Wares, Inc. Buffalo, NY, 2003.

Winfield, Mason, *Spirits of the Great Hill*, Western New York Wares, Inc. Buffalo, NY, 2001.

Winfield, Mason. *Village of Ghosts of Western New York*, Western New York Wares, Inc. Buffalo, NY, 2006.

Winfield, Mason, Shadows of the Western Door, Western New York Wares, Inc. Buffalo, NY, 1997.

Winfield, Mason, *Ghosts of 1812*, Petit Printing Corporation, Buffalo, NY, 2009.

White, Truman C. *History of Lancaster, NY,* The Boston History Co. http://history.rays-place.com/ny/lancaster-ny.htm, 1898.

USS *Sullivans*, http://en.wikipedia.org/wiki/Japanese_submarine_I-26. Accessed 2009

USS *Sullivans*, http://en.wikipedia.org/wiki/USS_Juneau_(CL-52). Accessed 2009.

Voelkl, Jeffery F. "Williamsville Water Mill." *Amherst Bee.* January 21, 2009.

Vogt, Evon Z and Hyman, Ray. *Water Witching USA*. The University of Chicago Press, Chicago, IL, 1959.

Zaffis, John. Lecture, Lily Dale Assemble, 2007.

Zaffis, John. *Shadows of the Dark*, iUniverse, Inc., Lincoln, NW, 2004.

Zagora, Robert. Interview by Rev. T. Shaw, July, 2007.